Published by Eagle Publications
P O Box 73374, London W3 3FZ, England.
A Paperback Original

First published in the United Kingdom in 2020

Text copyright © 2020 Roselle Thompson

The right of Roselle Thompson to be identified as the Author
of this work has been asserted by her.

Cover design by V3Creative Designs

ISBN 978-1-8381068-0-5
A CIP catalogue record for this book is available from the British Library

All Rights Reserved

This book is sold subject to the condition that it shall not, by way of trade or otherwise, be lent, hired out or otherwise circulated in any form of binding or cover other than that in which it is published. No part of this publication may be reproduced, stored in a retrieval system, or transmitted in any form or by any means (electronic, mechanical, photocopying, recording or otherwise) without the prior written permission of Eagle Publications.

All paper used by Eagle Publications is SFI (Sustainable Forestry Initiative) and PEFC (Programme for the Endorsement of Forest Certification Schemes) Certified.

This is a work of fiction. Names, characters, incidents and dialogues are products of the author's imagination or are used fictitiously. Any resemblance to actual people, living or dead, events or locales is entirely coincidental.

Printed in the United Kingdom and United States by

Lightning Source for Eagle Publishers

www.eaglepublications.co.uk

EAGLE PUBLICATIONS

Who is the 11+ English Preparation Tests for the CEM-style Test for?

About the 11+ Tests

Preparing for the 11+ entrance examinations can be challenging for both children and their parents. One of the first things to know is that the content of the 11+ exams changes from year to year. Additionally, the level and pass mark requirement on a given year may differ from county to county. The 11+ tests are selection tests are set by GL Assessment (NFER), CEM (The University of Durham) or individual schools may set their entrance own tests. This book has been written to develop literacy and reasoning skills and is specifically aimed at:

- ❖ Those taking the 11+ papers
- ❖ Grammar school Entrance tests
- ❖ Independent Secondary School entrance tests
- ❖ Those considering taking Scholarship papers

Although the Practice tests are designed to reflect the style of the CEM tests, it also provides suitable preparation for all 11+ tests in general.

The CEM Test

First of all, there are two papers. The exams are separated into timed sections which are delivered by audio instructions. In each paper children's abilities are tested in verbal reasoning, non-verbal reasoning and numerical reasoning. Therefore this book is intended to help your child practice in English, for the test and to identify areas of strength and weakness, whilst developing exam techniques for success.

Subject areas covered in this book

- ➤ **Comprehension – multiple choice**
- ➤ **Shuffled sentences**
- ➤ **Synonyms**
- ➤ **Cloze sentences**
- ➤ **Grammar**
- ➤ **Antonyms**

About this book

- ✓ This book will help you to get used to answering questions for your CEM test
- ✓ Practice working within time limits
- ✓ Help you gain confidence to take the test
- ✓ Plan to work on weak areas and practice problem areas
- ✓ Use the results in these tests to identify areas where you may need further help
- ✓ Talk about the upcoming test and learn that doing your best is what really matters.
- ✓ Your child should aim to score at least 75% if they score less than this, use the results to work out where more practice is needed.
- ✓ Progress check – Keep a track of your scores, using the progress chart inside the back cover of this book.

PLEASE NOTE: *CEM* stands for Centre for Evaluation and Monitoring, Durham University and the University of Durham, which are all trademarks of the University of Durham.
This Phoenix Study Guide is not associated with CEM or the University of Durham in any way. This book does not include any official questions and it is not endorsed by CEM or the University of Durham.

Phoenix Study Guides

11+ EXAMS - ENGLISH PRACTICE TEST PAPERS

**CEM STYLE
ENGLISH TESTS**

By

Roselle Thompson

This Book Belongs to:

Name: ....

Contents

There are 5 Exam style Practice Test Papers included in this book.

Each test is designed to cover a good range of question styles and topics. *An Answer Sheet for each test is also included*.
There is Guidance for parents as well as Instructions on how to complete and mark the tests

- ✓ **Test Paper 1** — page 1
- ✓ **Test Answer Sheet** — page 21
- ✓ **Test Paper 2** — page 22
- ✓ **Test Answer Sheet** — page 42
- ✓ **Test Paper 3** — page 43
- ✓ **Test Answer Sheet** — page 63
- ✓ **Test Paper 4** — page 64
- ✓ **Test Answer Sheet** — page 84
- ✓ **Test Paper 5** — page 85
- ✓ **Test Answer Sheet** — page 105
- ✓ **Answers for all tests - 1 to 5** — page 106-115

Guidance for parents

What is needed to sit these test papers

- Choose a place that is quiet
- Make sure there is a clock that is visible
- A pencil and a rubber
- A piece of paper
- Remember no dictionary or thesaurus is allowed

Taking the test

- ✓ Do not talk to your child during the test; wait until the test is over to talk about areas in the test that they found difficult
- ✓ Cut out the answers and keep them hidden from your child
- ✓ Tear out the answer sheet section, your child will need to write his/her name on the top of the first answer sheet.
- ✓ When your child is ready, let them begin Test Paper 1
- ✓ Ask your child to go through the examples at the start of each section of the practice Test.
- ✓ Your child must write the answers clearly on the Answer Sheet
- ✓ Once the test is over, you can both go through the questions that were incorrect.

Completing the Answer Sheet

- DO NOT write the answers on the question paper; use the Answer sheet for answers.
- Put a horizontal line through the boxes on the answer sheet.
- If you want to change an answer, using your rubber, erase the incorrect answer and then select the new answer.
- Remember all rough workings should be done on a separate piece of paper.

Reading the symbols at the foot the page

You will see written instructions at the start of each section of the test and also at the foot of the page. Your child must follow these instructions.

At the foot of the page you will see this sign; it means you must continue working.

You must stop and wait for instructions when you see this one

(c) 2020 Roselle Thompson11+ Exam English Preparation Tests

The Instructions at the beginning of each section

There are instructions at the beginning of each section. Your child should be aware of the time allowed for the test; how many questions there are and how to complete the answers.

Read the examples at the beginning of every section, which shows the type of questions that are included in the section.

Time Management

The tests provide essential practice of the types of questions that could arise in the CEM test. They are designed to help your child practise and work at managing their time.

Marking the Test Papers

Score each question with **1** mark

Your child should be aiming for 70% or more at the beginning of the test papers and at least 75% or more in the weeks leading up to the exam.

If your child does not score a good mark, continue to provide a variety of practice questions to widen your child's knowledge.

Focus on areas that show weak performance. Remember, the content of the CEM exams vary from year to year; therefore, a good score in this test paper does not guarantee a pass. In fact, a lower score may not always suggest a fail, so talk to your child, let them know that doing their best is really what matters, as they gain confidence in their abilities.

CEM is Centre for Evaluation and Monitoring and the University of Durham are all trademarks of the University of Durham.

PLEASE NOTE that Eagle Publications is not associated with CEM or the University of Durham in any way. Also note that this book does not contain any official questions and it is not endorsed by CEM or the Univesity of Durham.

The questions here are based on those set by CEM, but we cannot guarantee that your child's actual 11+ exams will contain the same question types or format as this book.

Test Paper 1

Instructions:

1. Make sure you have pencils and an eraser for this test.
2. You must be able to see a clock or watch.
3. Write your name on the answer sheet.
4. Do not open the question booklet until you are told to do so by the audio instructions.
5. You must listen carefully to the audio instructions given.
6. Mark your answers on the answer sheet only.
7. All workings must be completed on a separate piece of paper.
8. Do not use a calculator, dictionary or thesaurus at any time in the test.
9. Be sure you move through the tests as quickly as possible, but with care.
10. Follow the instructions at the foot of each page.
11. Mark your answers with a horizontal strike, as shown on the answer sheet.
12. If you want to change your answer make sure you rub out your first answer and that your second answer is clearly visible.
13. You can go back and review any questions that are within the section you are working on only.
14. You must wait for further instructions before you move on to another question.

SYMBOLS AND PHRASES USED IN THE TESTS

  Instructions

  Time allowed for this section

  Stop and wait for further instructions

  Continue working

Comprehension

INSTRUCTIONS

YOU HAVE **9** MINUTES TO COMPLETE THE FOLLOWING SECTION

YOU HAVE **10** QUESTIONS TO COMPLETE WITHIN THE TIME GIVEN.

EXAMPLE

Comprehension Example

Before the dreadful accident, the train with its torn seats had rusty window frames and a multitude of spots of chewing gum which covered its worn-out floors. Now looking at the mangled wreck, passengers, who complained about the strange metallic smell, were lucky to have escaped with no injuries.

Example 1

According to the passage, what seems to have had happened to the train?

A It was dirty
B It was unpleasant to ride in
C It was involved in an accident
D It was scrapped as it was old

The correct answer is C.

STOP AND WAIT FOR FURTHER INSTRUCTIONS

The Fugitive

This was a moment he had visualised during the many years that he was trapped and tortured by his foreign captors. They had concluded that he could not speak their language, when he refused to answer every single one of their questions. This tactic had, in turn, forced him into a world of silence, which was made more torturous over the past five years. Would he be able to speak his own language again? The truth is, he had understood every word they had spoken; especially their plan to execute him in secret, with a conspiracy to claim he had committed suicide. That was the moment when his escape plan was hatched. He needed to stay alive. He needed to see his family again. He needed to tell the world his story.

The bongo drum returned to beat louder in his chest and its rising crescendo instilled by fear, jerked him out of his moment's reverie back to reality. He could feel the panic rising in his body as the echo of his friend's voice returned to spur him on, *"Run Charlie, Run! Go West!"* Immediately, his legs became wheels that drove themselves. He didn't mind getting soaked as his body propelled him to his expected place of safety. Beads of sweat mingled with the drizzling rain, and he ran like a hare, being pursued by a fox in the shadows of the overhanging leafy trees.

The rain fell heavier, as he headed in one direction guided only by instincts. Although he had been travelling for a while now, he was aware that his pursuers could be in vehicles and they would be much faster than him. He immediately dismissed the idea. No time for such thoughts, he told himself. He was, he assumed, heading *West*, just as Miguel, his friend, had advised; into the direction of the setting sun and the pale orange sky. The autumn wind blew cool, making his soaked clothes feel cold. Despite this he had one single objective; to reach the place of safety, where he was assured by Miguel, he would be given assistance to escape from the island by boat.

He could hear faint sounds of wailing sirens in the far distance; they were not close but hearing them caused his nervous stomach to perform fearful somersaults in his belly. He must be patient, *"West"* was where Miguel had come from and he had spoken of nothing but his beloved home, a place of gentle and loving people, with hearts of gold, Miguel had emphasised; except, for the fact that he was cruelly framed and sent to jail for something he had not done.

Night was falling fast and he would soon need to rest. He needed food and a drink; there was none. He had smoked his last cigarette butt hours ago, and had no real way of protecting himself in the open woodland at night. It was a case of mind over matter and having made it thus far, he had to remain focus on reaching his destination by going *"West"*.

Miguel, his deceased friend, had been his cell mate; a fellow prisoner, who had insisted throughout the five years they spent together, that he was innocent. He had visualised escaping too, in order to prove his innocence. Sadly, he contracted lung cancer and died a horrible, painful death. Life, he said, had been unkind to him.

"But you Charlie, you must succeed. You have to tell my story - clear my name," were Miguel's last and dying words.

CONTINUE WORKING

Those words became Charlie's driving force, they constantly echoed in his head. Finally, he selected a spot to rest for the night and there he lay, curled up like a foetus, forcing his body to shape like a baby; wishing his tired body could comfort him. Sleep came immediately, and he drifted off, extremely exhausted but glad that for now, he seemed to have evaded his captors. Charlie went to sleep not know what the night would bring, but he was hopeful for a chance to fulfil his and Miguel's mission.

Questions

1. What does the phrase "*a moment he had visualised*" mean?
    A. Realise
    B. Predicted
    C. Imagined
    D. Anticipated
    E. frightened

2. Which word tells us that the narrator is not in his home town?
    A. Woodland
    B. Foreign
    C. West
    D. Echoed
    E. run

3. What is the meaning of the word *"tactic"* in *paragraph 1*?
    A. Organise
    B. Plan
    C. Wanted
    D. Report
    E. answer

4. What is the narrator's heartbeat compared to?
    A. Horns
    B. Sirens
    C. Drums
    D. Rainfall
    E. Voices

5. Although Charlie pretended not to understand his captors, which word in *paragraph 1* made him realise he was going to die?
    A. Dead
    B. Execute
    C. Hang
    D. Kill
    E. Organise

CONTINUE WORKING

6. Which *Simile* describes the way that Charlie was running?
   A. Like a rabbit
   B. as a fox
   C. Like a hare
   D. As rain
   E. Like wheels

7. What was the weather during the narrator's escape like?
   A. Sunny
   B. Snowing
   C. Hailing
   D. Stormy
   E. Raining

8. What did the narrator rely on to find his way during his escape?
   A. A map
   B. His friend's voice
   C. His instincts
   D. His compass
   E. What he remembered

9. What does the word *"deceased"* in *paragraph 6* mean?
   A. Stop what you are doing
   B. Dead
   C. Prohibit
   D. Alive
   E. Sick

10. What was the cause of Miguel's death?
    A. He was executed
    B. Fell into a hole
    C. Caught the flu
    D. He had lung cancer
    E. He died of old age

STOP AND WAIT FOR FURTHER INSTRUCTIONS

Shuffled Sentences

INSTRUCTIONS

YOU HAVE **8** MINUTES TO COMPLETE THE FOLLOWING SECTION

YOU HAVE **15** QUESTIONS TO COMPLETE WITHIN THE TIME GIVEN.

EXAMPLES

Example 1

The following sentence is shuffled and also contains one unnecessary word. Rearrange the sentence correctly in order to identify the unnecessary word.

Train did time on arrive is not the ran.

A	B	C	D	E
work	ran	morning	try	office

The correct answer is B.

Example 2

Someone door the waited the rang for they to farm open bell and

A	B	C	D	E
home	stood	closed	farm	inside

The correct answer is D.

STOP AND WAIT FOR FURTHER INSTRUCTIONS

Shuffled Sentences

These sentences are shuffled and also contain one unnecessary word. Rearrange them correctly in order to identify the word that's unnecessary.

1. Had weather barbecue the despite of forecast wet we dry still a.

A	B	C	D	E
weather	dry	despite	wet	forecast

2. Film the booked tickets see latest home we to.

A	B	C	D	E
home	tickets	film	booked	see

3. The for dog although ran its to fetch stick for owner the.

A	B	C	D	E
fetch	owner	dog	stick	although

4. Damaged news The reported a had weather hurricane the island.

A	B	C	D	E
a	weather	the	damaged	reported

5. Interview so time He was late catch for bus so he ran the his.

A	B	C	D	E
so	for	the	time	to

6. A Many boat tourists the cruise went took river on Thames.

A	B	C	D	E
the	took	many	the	a

7. Dog at the day black cat barked the neighbour's playful.

A	B	C	D	E
day	black	the	playful	at

CONTINUE WORKING

8. Bathroom our we had builder a new in shower installed.

A	B	C	D	E
new	builder	had	our	in

9. Pillows by she uncomfortable sat up two bed propped in

A	B	C	D	E
bed	in	propped	up	uncomfortable

10. Cried the screamed on loudly the scary ride children.

A	B	C	D	E
scary	cried	loudly	the	on

11. Rider the horse fast trotted around with the field its new.

A	B	C	D	E
fast	new	the	around	with

12. Broke the ball garden boy kicked window the which his neighbour's.

A	B	C	D	E
broke	the	garden	his	which

13. On an accident heavy caused a traffic the jam motorway.

A	B	C	D	E
jam	heavy	a	motorway	the

14. Monarch the current England British Queen Elizabeth II is .

A	B	C	D	E
England	British	the	Queen	current

15. In looked the vase flowers bright beautiful glass in their.

A	B	C	D	E
glass	the	in	bright	beautiful

STOP AND WAIT FOR FURTHER INSTRUCTIONS

Synonyms

 **INSTRUCTIONS**

 YOU HAVE **7** MINUTES TO COMPLETE THE FOLLOWING SECTION

YOU HAVE **24** QUESTIONS TO COMPLETE WITHIN THE TIME GIVEN.

EXAMPLES

Example 1

Select the word that is most similar in meaning to the following word:

tranquil

A	B	C	D	E
rowdy	windy	quite	peaceful	reach

*The correct answer is **D**.*

Example 2

Select the word that is most similar in meaning to the following word:

humorous

A	B	C	D	E
humble	peculiar	holy	comic	creative

*The correct answer is **C**.*

STOP AND WAIT FOR FURTHER INSTRUCTIONS

Synonyms

There are 24 questions to complete in this time. You have 7 minutes to complete this section.

Select the word from the table that is most similar in meaning to the word above the table.

1. OPAQUE

A	B	C	D	E
transparent	advance	blurred	oppress	solemn

2. SERENE

A	B	C	D	E
cautious	calm	intense	incite	rapid

3. COMMENCE

A	B	C	D	E
oppress	volatile	pointless	scarce	begin

4. FRAGILE

A	B	C	D	E
distinct	delicate	resource	magical	liable

5. FLEXIBLE

A	B	C	D	E
further	lucid	fallible	solvent	bendable

6. ABUNDANT

A	B	C	D	E
select	transcript	evaluate	lots	scarce

7. COMPLEX

A	B	C	D	E
intricate	noticeable	immense	maximum	complement

CONTINUE WORKING

8. INSPIRING

A	B	C	D	E
DETER	ESSENTIAL	ABSURD	INAUDIBLE	MOTIVATING

9. ADEQUATE

A	B	C	D	E
maintain	reaction	industrious	hinder	sufficient

10. DEPENDENT

A	B	C	D	E
preserve	rely	absurd	unwise	reaction

11. ENCHANTED

A	B	C	D	E
repulsive	fright	suspicious	fascinated	folly

12. INSOLENT

A	B	C	D	E
disdain	awkward	rude	dense	clear

13. VELOCITY

A	B	C	D	E
simple	success	speed	hinder	laziness

14. IMITATE

A	B	C	D	E
encourage	deter	mimic	thrive	preserve

15. OPTIMISTIC

A	B	C	D	E
reaction	icon	significance	motion	positive

CONTINUE WORKING

16. DECEIVE

A	B	C	D	E
placid	cunning	calm	inflexible	evaluate

17. CONFESS

A	B	C	D	E
culprit	subtract	declare	speak	affect

18. WRATH

A	B	C	D	E
sad	anger	devout	tame	affable

19. MULTITUDE

A	B	C	D	E
suitable	madness	crowd	crate	delighted

20. SERENE

A	B	C	D	E
strong	proof	adapt	twisted	peaceful

21. DISPERSE

A	B	C	D	E
unjust	gather	congregate	scatter	extract

22. EVADE

A	B	C	D	E
catch	react	dodge	absurd	essential

23. AMIABLE

A	B	C	D	E
deceitful	aggressive	friendly	unwise	follower

24. REMEDY

A	B	C	D	E
liquid	substance	cure	difference	remain

STOP AND WAIT FOR FURTHER INSTRUCTIONS

Grammar

⚠️ **INSTRUCTIONS**

🕐 **YOU HAVE 5 MINUTES TO COMPLETE THE FOLLOWING SECTION**

YOU HAVE 8 QUESTIONS TO COMPLETE WITHIN THE TIME GIVEN.

EXAMPLES

Example 1 - Select the word from the boxes below that is *misspelt*

A	B	C	D	E
lifes	open	sweet	repeat	bishop

The correct answer is A.

Example 2 - Select the correct prefix or suffix below to give the opposite to the word *mature.*

A	B	C	D	E
in	il	im	re	non

The correct answer is C.

STOP AND WAIT FOR FURTHER INSTRUCTIONS

1. Select the homophone of the word **"so"** from the words below.

A	B	C	D	E
Show	Sew	See	sown	low

2. Select the word below that is misspelt.

A	B	C	D	E
reign	curiousity	brief	allow	wrath

3. Identify the homograph of the word **"waste"**

A	B	C	D	E
bow	try	fry	waist	tyre

4. Select the word that is misspelt

A	B	C	D	E
aquire	simile	whom	correct	waiter

5. Identify the homonym of the word **"feeble"**

A	B	C	D	E
bright	fragile	feather	strong	frown

6. Select the word that is misspelt

A	B	C	D	E
egsample	collar	practice	bough	break

7. Identify the synonym of the word **"jovial"**

A	B	C	D	E
real	fearful	strong	happy	leader

8. Identify the word that is misspelt

A	B	C	D	E
comittee	reality	favourite	trial	feather

STOP AND WAIT FOR FURTHER INSTRUCTIONS

Antonyms

 **INSTRUCTIONS**

 YOU HAVE **5** MINUTES TO COMPLETE THE FOLLOWING SECTION

YOU HAVE **15** QUESTIONS TO COMPLETE WITHIN THE TIME GIVEN.

EXAMPLES

Example 1

Which word is least similar to the following word:

dark

A	B	C	D	E
night	morning	light	bright	heavy

The correct answer is C.

Example 2

Which word is least similar to the following word:

departure

A	B	C	D	E
entrance	main	rough	arrival	below

The correct answer is D.

STOP AND WAIT FOR FURTHER INSTRUCTIONS

Choose a word from each box below, that is opposite to the word in the question:

1. *beneath*

A	B	C	D	E
far	distance	nearby	below	above

2. *victory*

A	B	C	D	E
defeat	celebrate	win	allow	happy

3. *opaque*

A	B	C	D	E
abundant	transparent	thick	trial	loose

4. *essential*

A	B	C	D	E
right	smart	reaction	unimportant	potential

5. *prohibit*

A	B	C	D	E
silence	reaction	allow	deny	available

6. *admiration*

A	B	C	D	E
scorn	success	motivate	preserve	awkward

7. *multitude*

A	B	C	D	E
individual	group	bunch	spectators	fans

8. *condone*

A	B	C	D	E
prohibit	discourage	agree	frank	innocent

CONTINUE WORKING

9. industrious

A	B	C	D	E
smart	polite	indolent	absurd	generous

10. thrifty

A	B	C	D	E
noticeable	common	spendthrift	presence	deter

11. ample

A	B	C	D	E
lots	scarce	wisdom	failure	anticipate

12. insolent

A	B	C	D	E
unwise	selfish	frank	polite	prevent

13. adhere

A	B	C	D	E
disobey	humorous	admit	follow	narrow

14. vicinity

A	B	C	D	E
common	cunning	absurd	distant	space

15. audible

A	B	C	D	E
automatic	noticeable	inaudible	speciality	suspicious

STOP AND WAIT FOR FURTHER INSTRUCTIONS

(c) 2020 Roselle Thompson   *11+ Exam English Preparation Tests*

Cloze

 **INSTRUCTIONS**

 **YOU HAVE 10 MINUTES TO COMPLETE THE FOLLOWING SECTION**

YOU HAVE 20 QUESTIONS TO COMPLETE WITHIN THE TIME GIVEN.

EXAMPLES

Example 1

Read the sentence below and select the most appropriate word from the table.

A	B	C	D	E
canopy	canvas	scenery	display	picture

The wall of the abandoned building was the perfect ....for the painter.

Example 2

Read the sentence below and select the most appropriate word from the table.

A	B	C	D	E
send	call	attend	reply	absent

We are expected to ....to the wedding invitation before the end of the month.

STOP AND WAIT FOR FURTHER INSTRUCTIONS

Read the passage and select the most appropriate word from the table below.

A	B	C	D	E
ledges	structure	first	mystery	Archaeologists

F	G	H	I	J
buried	Wonders	paintings	sides	existence

Ancient Egypt Pyramids

Many people are amazed by the (Q1) .... of the Ancient Egyptian pyramids that were built by humans in ancient times. These giant structures were built as burial places for their Pharaohs or Kings, who were (Q2) ....with all sorts of items and treasure. This is because the Egyptian people believed that the Pharaoh needed certain things to survive in the afterlife. The walls of the pyramids were often covered with carvings and (Q3)............................ Near to the Pharaoh's burial chamber would be other rooms where family members and servants were buried.

There are different types of pyramids; some of the earlier ones were called step pyramids because they have large (Q4).....................that look like giant steps. Some (Q5) .... think that the steps were the stairways for the Pharaoh to climb to the sun god. Later pyramids had more sloping and flat (Q6)............................ It is believed that the sun god stood on these pyramids and created the other gods and goddesses.

The enormous size of the pyramids is a (Q7) ....to many people today. There are approximately 140 Egyptian pyramids – some are huge and the biggest is the Pyramid of Khufu; also called the Great Pyramid of Giza. The Great Pyramid of Giza was over 480 feet tall when it was (Q8) .... built. In fact, it was the tallest man-made (Q9) .... for nearly 4,000 years. Today, it is considered as one of the Seven (Q10) .... of the World.

CONTINUE WORKING

Read the passage and select the most appropriate word from the table below.

A	B	C	D	E
buzz	curious	London	diversity	designer

F	G	H	I	J
Doomsday	memorable	discoveries	stroll	antiques

Saturday and Sunday Markets in England

Markets are (Q11) ....places to buy a variety of things from open-air, local, street- vendors in pop-up gazebo spaces, who will be out in force, selling everything from hand-made jewellery, cutting edge (Q12) ....and ex-designer goods, to a wide variety of stalls and shops with hand-crafted, recycled items for the home, quirky perfumes, organic fruit and vegetables, fresh fish, meat, and all types of seafood, impressive (Q13)................., occasional rare furniture and (Q14) ....items of memorabilia.

Some of the most famous (Q15).......................Markets are Spitalfields, Camden, Greenwich and Portobello. Interestingly, the first written record of a market in Norwich, for instance, dates back to 1086 (Q16).......................Book record, which is evidence of quite a history of market wheeling and dealing!

As you (Q17) ....around the London market squares, the (Q18) ....in the air from the independent traders reflect a (Q19) ...., that combines a variety of history and cultures, dress, music and styles; as you barter for affordable little (Q20) ....and items that won't break your bank.

STOP AND WAIT FOR FURTHER INSTRUCTIONS

Answer Sheet - Paper 1

COMPREHENSION						SYNONYMS Continued						SYNONYMS Continued						GRAMMAR					
1	A	B	C	D	E	10	A	B	C	D	E	20	A	B	C	D	E	1	A	B	C	D	E
2	A	B	C	D	E	11	A	B	C	D	E	21	A	B	C	D	E	2	A	B	C	D	E
3	A	B	C	D	E	12	A	B	C	D	E	22	A	B	C	D	E	3	A	B	C	D	E
4	A	B	C	D	E	13	A	B	C	D	E	23	A	B	C	D	E	4	A	B	C	D	E
5	A	B	C	D	E	14	A	B	C	D	E	24	A	B	C	D	E	5	A	B	C	D	E
6	A	B	C	D	E	15	A	B	C	D	E							6	A	B	C	D	E
7	A	B	C	D	E	16	A	B	C	D	E							7	A	B	C	D	E
8	A	B	C	D	E	17	A	B	C	D	E							8	A	B	C	D	E
9	A	B	C	D	E	18	A	B	C	D	E												
10	A	B	C	D	E	19	A	B	C	D	E												

SHUFFLED SENTENCES						ANTONYMS						CLOZE – you will need to choose from these LETTERS: A B C D E F G H I J											
1	A	B	C	D	E	1	A	B	C	D	E	1						16					
2	A	B	C	D	E	2	A	B	C	D	E	2						17					
3	A	B	C	D	E	3	A	B	C	D	E	3						18					
4	A	B	C	D	E	4	A	B	C	D	E	4						19					
5	A	B	C	D	E	5	A	B	C	D	E	5						20					
6	A	B	C	D	E	6	A	B	C	D	E	6											
7	A	B	C	D	E	7	A	B	C	D	E	7											
8	A	B	C	D	E	8	A	B	C	D	E	8											
9	A	B	C	D	E	9	A	B	C	D	E	9											
10	A	B	C	D	E	10	A	B	C	D	E	10											
11	A	B	C	D	E	11	A	B	C	D	E	11											
12	A	B	C	D	E	12	A	B	C	D	E	12											
13	A	B	C	D	E	13	A	B	C	D	E	13											
14	A	B	C	D	E	14	A	B	C	D	E	14											
15	A	B	C	D	E	15	A	B	C	D	E	15											

SYNONYMS					
1	A	B	C	D	E
2	A	B	C	D	E
3	A	B	C	D	E
4	A	B	C	D	E
5	A	B	C	D	E
6	A	B	C	D	E
7	A	B	C	D	E
8	A	B	C	D	E
9	A	B	C	D	E

Shade the correct answer box
If the answer is **D** then shade **D**:

Example:

A	B	C	D

Test Paper 2

Instructions:

1. Make sure you have pencils and an eraser for this test.
2. You must be able to see a clock or watch.
3. Write your name on the answer sheet.
4. Do not open the question booklet until you are told to do so by the audio instructions.
5. You must listen carefully to the audio instructions given.
6. Mark your answers on the answer sheet only.
7. All workings must be completed on a separate piece of paper.
8. Do not use a calculator, dictionary or thesaurus at any time in the test.
9. Be sure you move through the tests as quickly as possible, but with care.
10. Follow the instructions at the foot of each page.
11. Mark your answers with a horizontal strike, as shown on the answer sheet.
12. If you want to change your answer make sure you rub out your first answer and that your second answer is clearly visible.
13. You can go back and review any questions that are within the section you are working on only.
14. You must wait for further instructions before you move on to another question.

SYMBOLS AND PHRASES USED IN THE TESTS

 Instructions

 Time allowed for this section

 Stop and wait for further instructions

 Continue working

Comprehension

INSTRUCTIONS

YOU HAVE 9 MINUTES TO COMPLETE THE FOLLOWING SECTION

YOU HAVE 10 QUESTIONS TO COMPLETE WITHIN THE TIME GIVEN.

EXAMPLE

Comprehension Example

Before the dreadful accident, the train with its torn seats had rusty window frames and a multitude of spots of chewing gum which covered its worn-out floors. Now looking at the mangled wreck, passengers, who complained about the strange metallic smell, were lucky to have escaped with no injuries.

Example 1

According to the passage, what seems to have had happened to the train?

A   It was dirty
B   It was unpleasant to ride in
C   It was involved in an accident
D   It was scrapped as it was old

The correct answer is C.

STOP AND WAIT FOR FURTHER INSTRUCTIONS

The Golden Gate Bridge

History has shown that as cities develop and businesses grow, there are usually other growing needs, such as the demand for faster and reliable means of moving from one place to another. This was the situation before the construction of the Golden Gate Bridge in San Francisco, California, in the early 20th century. San Francisco was one of the fastest developing cities in the United States, but with a lack of quick, reliable transportation, the city's growth slowed down and even stopped. The existing popular ferry service at that time was not enough, so travellers demanded a bridge that could make travel easier and quicker. Such a bridge would need to cover a three-mile-long and one-mile wide body of water that connects the Pacific Ocean to the San Francisco Bay. One of the first ideas was to construct a gigantic suspension bridge over Fort Point at the tip of the Golden Gate Strait. It wasn't until 1916, that James Wilkins, a former engineering student, created a feasible proposal for a complicated bridge that would cost around $100 million, (approximately $2 billion in today's money).

Before the Golden Gate Bridge was constructed, many had thought it was not only dangerous but impossible to build a bridge that would connect the Marin Headlands to the city of San Francisco. Much of the fear at that time was due to the concerns of many engineers and architects, who believed it was impossible to build a bridge over such a long channel. Logically, there were also queries about building the bridge because of the strong tides, deep water (372 feet at its deepest) and heavy outbursts of wind and fog, that would make constructing such a long bridge difficult. In fact, many people had scoffed at the idea until an engineer and poet, Joseph Strauss, believed that such a project was indeed feasible. And although there were objections from ferry services who that saw this bridge-building idea as competition, Strauss with his team of engineers, began constructing the bridge in 1933.

To deal with some of the dangers of construction, Strauss had an idea to hang a huge safety net under the bridge so that if workers fell, they would be saved from dying in the cold Pacific Ocean. However, despite having this safety net, 11 men died during the project; one fell past the net and 10 others perished when a chunk of scaffolding fell with them and destroyed the safety barrier. The loss of life was tragic but many consoled themselves with the fact that given the enormity of the construction project, the figure of only 11 deaths was regarded as a huge achievement, because construction work at the time was extremely dangerous. It is not known precisely how many people worked on the £35 million project, but the bridge was finally completed on 27th May 1937.

At the time it was built, the Golden Gate Bridge was the longest suspension bridge in the world, until in 1964, a longer bridge, the *Verrazano-Narrows Bridge* in New York City, was built. Since then, these bridges have had greater competition from today's longest suspension bridge in the world – *the Akashi Kaikyo Bridge* in Japan, which is 3,911m long.

The Golden Gate Bridge was finally opened on 27th May, with an opening celebration, that lasted for longer than a week. Over 200,000 people crossed the bridge, before traffic was finally allowed on it. Today, the 2.7km (8,981ft) bridge, with its official colour known as International Orange, stands as an example of great human creativity, talent and intelligence.

CONTINUE WORKING

Questions

1. **What situations encouraged the construction of the Golden Bridge?**
   a. People wanted to ride on a bridge
   b. People moved from place to place
   c. People demanded a quicker and efficient method of travelling
   d. Businesses wanted to get bigger

2. **What did San Francisco desperately need as it expanded as a city?**
   a. More businesses growth and expansion
   b. More people to travel to its city
   c. Reliable methods of travelling to help its growth
   d. A ferry service to make travel easier and faster

3. **Circle two facts that are TRUE about San Francisco**
   a. San Francisco is a US city which grew fast then slowed down
   b. It is a very busy city that is located in New York
   c. The city developed rapidly during the early 20th century
   d. The ferry service in San Francisco was adequate for its needs

4. **What was the most challenging situation in San Francisco at that time?**
   a. Swimming over a 3 mile long by one mile wide body of water
   b. Building a colossal bridge connecting the Paciffic Ocean to San Francisco Bay
   c. The loss of life when building the Golden Gate Bridge
   d. Workers who were sick whilst building the bridge

5. **What was perhaps the most challenging concern in building the bridge?**
   a. The bridge would collapse with too much weight on it
   b. The sea water and strong tides would be a huge problem
   c. People would fall into the sea and drown
   d. No one had the intelligence to build the bridge

6. **Circle statements that are TRUE about the Golden Gate Bridge**
   a. The bridge was built over approximately 372 ft of deep sea water
   b. Constructing the bridge was not so difficult after all
   c. The government saved $100 million dollars after the bridge was built
   d. The bridge engineer was a poet

7. **Who first created a workable plan for building the bridge?**
   a. Johnson Strauss
   b. Johan Strauss
   c. Jonathan Straus
   d. Joseph Strauss

CONTINUE WORKING

8. **How many people worked on the Bridge project?**
   a. 35 million people worked on the bridge project
   b. Three thousand nine hundred and 11 people worked on the projecct
   c. No one knows how many people worked on the bridge project
   d. Over 20,000 people worked on the bridge project

9. **Why it was still considered a huge achievement that 11 men died during the bridge-building project?**
   a. The men were very old when they died
   b. The size of the bridge building project was huge compared with the few deaths that occured
   c. The men were not cautious enough, so they met tragic deaths
   d. The workers caught the cold from the cold Pacific Ocean

10. **Why is the Golden Gate Bridge no longer the longest suspension bridge in the world?**
    a. The size of the bridge started shrinking from 27th May 1937 to date
    b. Too many people walked on the bridge when it was opened
    c. Other bridges have been built which are much longer than Golden Gate
    d. Its International Orange colour makes it seem smaller when you look at it in the sun.

STOP AND WAIT FOR FURTHER INSTRUCTIONS

Shuffled Sentences

 **INSTRUCTIONS**

 YOU HAVE **8** MINUTES TO COMPLETE THE FOLLOWING SECTION

YOU HAVE **15** QUESTIONS TO COMPLETE WITHIN THE TIME GIVEN.

EXAMPLES

Example 1

The following sentence is shuffled and also contains one unnecessary word. Rearrange the sentence correctly in order to identify the unnecessary word.

Train did time on arrive is not the ran.

A	B	C	D	E
work	ran	morning	try	office

The correct answer is B.

Example 2

Someone door the waited the rang for they to farm open bell and

A	B	C	D	E
home	stood	closed	farm	inside

The correct answer is D.

STOP AND WAIT FOR FURTHER INSTRUCTIONS

Shuffled Sentences

These sentences are shuffled and also contain one unnecessary word. Rearrange them correctly in order to identify the word that's unnecessary.

1. All they virus get because shops of dangerous a closed the.

A	B	C	D	E
the	of	get	all	a

2. Train up 8pm clock Tom the from picked Mary station clock.

A	B	C	D	E
from	up	the		clock

3. Local my in dogs his two for neighbour park walked our.

A	B	C	D	E
in	for	his	our	my

4. When floor into the it broken glass the hit shattered floor fragments.

A	B	C	D	E
broken	it	hit	the	glass

5. Man centre the for called they sick home the in ambulance the.

A	B	C	D	E
the	in	man	home	they

6. Allowed did to we school our to were play we homework our only.

A	B	C	D	E
did	school	we	did	our

7. Looked the beautiful colourful the in garden rain rainbow flowers.

A	B	C	D	E
rainbow	in	looked	the	flowers

CONTINUE WORKING

8. Market the closed of because the Council windy local outdoor the weather.

A	B	C	D	E
of	the	local	closed	market

9. Strong bought bike for her lock at gym locker Jane a.

A	B	C	D	E
her	a	for	lock	bike

10. Station pick went from local blue his Ivan to up car the garage.

A	B	C	D	E
went	up	car	station	from

11. Faces whole so laughed cry funny made the class Jack.

A	B	C	D	E
whole	cry	made	the	whole

12. Coins soft the behind we sofa behind many grey room.

A	B	C	D	E
room	we	sofa	soft	the

13. On peas the cried her want plate green because did eat she to not she.

A	B	C	D	E
she	not	eat	green	cried

14. Cross her made Sarah on when her did clean mum room she not.

A	B	C	D	E
her	did	on	not	made

15. Special for vase apologised ancient mum's breaking Chinese he .

A	B	C	D	E
He	For	Special	base	ancient

STOP AND WAIT FOR FURTHER INSTRUCTIONS

Synonyms

 **INSTRUCTIONS**

 **YOU HAVE 7 MINUTES TO COMPLETE THE FOLLOWING SECTION**

YOU HAVE **24** QUESTIONS TO COMPLETE WITHIN THE TIME GIVEN.

EXAMPLES

Example 1

Select the word that is most similar in meaning to the following word:

tranquil

A	B	C	D	E
rowdy	windy	quite	peaceful	reach

The correct answer is D.

Example 2

Select the word that is most similar in meaning to the following word:

humorous

A	B	C	D	E
humble	peculiar	holy	comic	creative

The correct answer is C.

STOP AND WAIT FOR FURTHER INSTRUCTIONS

Synonyms

There are 24 questions to complete in this time. You have 7 minutes to complete this section.

Select the word from the table that is most similar in meaning to the word above the table.

1. ROBUST

A	B	C	D	E
Hesitate	rough	strong	caring	confess

2. CONCEAL

A	B	C	D	E
Ready	Comfortable	Rage	complex	hide

3. INDOLENT

A	B	C	D	E
happy	lazy	silent	truth	mockery

4. IMMINENT

A	B	C	D	E
inspire	depend	soon	praise	terminate

5. COMMENCE

A	B	C	D	E
begin	invade	tiring	opposite	disperse

6. HINDER

A	B	C	D	E
Reason	Fought	bravery	obstruct	consider

7. REVEAL

A	B	C	D	E
passion	helpful	show	tiring	strike

8. REMEDY

A	B	C	D	E
purpose	service	waste	cure	precious

CONTINUE WORKING

(c) 2020 Roselle Thompson *11+ Exam English Preparation Tests*

9. RAPID

A	B	C	D	E
delicate	fast	defy	courage	adore

10. PROHIBIT

A	B	C	D	E
challenge	adore	forbid	mystify	pure

11. YEARLY

A	B	C	D	E
bundle	imitate	emulate	annual	moment

12. AGILE

A	B	C	D	E
rare	merry	withdraw	anxious	flexible

13. NOISY

A	B	C	D	E
clench	rowdy	reason	repent	bicker

14. OPTION

A	B	C	D	E
indicate	contemplate	choice	fiery	loathe

15. WEAK

A	B	C	D	E
emotive	slumber	weary	feeble	imprint

16. VALOUR

A	B	C	D	E
bravery	imperative	confuse	imminent	guilt

17. SURRENDER

A	B	C	D	E
defiant	leave	yield	anxious	frighten

CONTINUE WORKING

18. UNITE

A	B	C	D	E
remain	false	unequal	join	split

19. STUBBORN

A	B	C	D	E
struggle	obstinate	reject	drain	jaded

20. OMINOUS

A	B	C	D	E
darkness	smear	omen	fever	soothe

21. VACANT

A	B	C	D	E
corrupt	inside	projected	empty	power

22. ROBUST

A	B	C	D	E
rumour	strong	hate	grave	expire

23. TRANQUIL

A	B	C	D	E
slowly	social	reverse	harmony	peaceful

24. STRINGENT

A	B	C	D	E
calm	wind	harsh	funny	sunny

STOP AND WAIT FOR FURTHER INSTRUCTIONS

Grammar

⚠ INSTRUCTIONS

🕐 YOU HAVE **5** MINUTES TO COMPLETE THE FOLLOWING SECTION

YOU HAVE **8** QUESTIONS TO COMPLETE WITHIN THE TIME GIVEN.

EXAMPLES

Example 1 - Select the word from the boxes below that is *misspelt*

A	B	C	D	E
lifes	open	sweet	repeat	bishop

*The correct answer is **A**.*

Example 2 - Select the correct *prefix or suffix* below to give the opposite to the word *mature.*

A	B	C	D	E
in	il	im	re	non

*The correct answer is **C**.*

STOP AND WAIT FOR FURTHER INSTRUCTIONS

(c) 2020 Roselle Thompson 　　　　　　　　　　　　　*11+ Exam English Preparation Tests*

1. Select the homophone of the word **"rein"** from the words below.

A	B	C	D	E
raw	reign	respect	rubbish	leave

2. Select the word below that is misspelt.

A	B	C	D	E
abilty	humour	tired	aloud	wrist

3. Identify the homograph of the word **"island"**.

A	B	C	D	E
irate	ilet	fragrant	weary	Ireland

4. Select the word that is misspelt.

A	B	C	D	E
acompany	confess	weary	peril	wrap

5. Identify the homonym of the word **"slender"**.

A	B	C	D	E
caring	feast	forget	slim	slow

6. Select the word that is misspelt.

A	B	C	D	E
exite	column	parade	bought	brisk

7. Identify the synonym of the word **"imitate"**.

A	B	C	D	E
sample	loud	single	copy	communicate

8. Identify the word that is misspelt.

A	B	C	D	E
generous	humoros	swimming	reveal	flexible

STOP AND WAIT FOR FURTHER INSTRUCTIONS

Antonyms

 **INSTRUCTIONS**

 **YOU HAVE 5 MINUTES TO COMPLETE THE FOLLOWING SECTION**

YOU HAVE 15 QUESTIONS TO COMPLETE WITHIN THE TIME GIVEN.

EXAMPLES

Example 1

Which word is least similar to the following word:

dark

A	B	C	D	E
night	morning	light	bright	heavy

The correct answer is C.

Example 2

Which word is least similar to the following word:

departure

A	B	C	D	E
entrance	main	rough	arrival	below

The correct answer is D.

STOP AND WAIT FOR FURTHER INSTRUCTIONS

(c) 2020 Roselle Thompson   *11+ Exam English Preparation Tests*

Choose a word from each box below, that is opposite to the word in the question:

1. real

A	B	C	D	E
near	disturb	simple	fake	right

2. curse

A	B	C	D	E
defiant	constant	couple	try	bless

3. reveal

A	B	C	D	E
hide	propose	penetrate	trust	might

4. war

A	B	C	D	E
pride	piece	peace	battle	weapon

5. stationary

A	B	C	D	E
slow	quickly	moving	disturb	static

6. allow

A	B	C	D	E
scary	prohibit	movement	attitude	honesty

7. disclose

A	B	C	D	E
clothing	close	secret	special	spectacular

8. hesitant

A	B	C	D	E
innocent	encourage	prompt	honest	sure

CONTINUE WORKING

9. permanent

A	B	C	D	E
small	temporary	hesitant	indolent	precious

10. loathe

A	B	C	D	E
knowledge	commuity	expansion	pretend	love

11. commence

A	B	C	D	E
end	half	commit	indignant	propose

12. modern

A	B	C	D	E
matrimony	mentor	mockery	previous	ancient

13. expand

A	B	C	D	E
contrast	contract	strong	stretch	narrow

14. active

A	B	C	D	E
atrocious	attentive	action	passive	proud

15. create

A	B	C	D	E
destroy	fashionable	creature	contrast	suspend

STOP AND WAIT FOR FURTHER INSTRUCTIONS

Cloze

⚠ INSTRUCTIONS

🕐 YOU HAVE **10** MINUTES TO COMPLETE THE FOLLOWING SECTION

YOU HAVE **20** QUESTIONS TO COMPLETE WITHIN THE TIME GIVEN.

EXAMPLES

Example 1

Read the sentence below and select the most appropriate word from the table.

A	B	C	D	E
canopy	canvas	scenery	display	picture

The wall of the abandoned building was the perfect ………………………….for the painter.

Example 2

Read the sentence below and select the most appropriate word from the table.

A	B	C	D	E
send	call	attend	reply	absent

We are expected to ……………………….to the wedding invitation before the end of the month.

STOP AND WAIT FOR FURTHER INSTRUCTIONS

Read the passage and select the most appropriate word from the table below.

A	B	C	D	E
species	branches	rainfall	undergrowth	surface

F	G	H	I	J
deforestation	temperate	hot	endangered	equator

Rainforests

Think about the word 'Rainforest' and two ideas should come to you; *rain* and *forest*! Therefore, just as the name suggests, rainforests are forests that grow in places in which there is a lot of (Q1)...................... In fact, the amount of rain that falls in such places is between 79 and 177 inches of rain (between 200cm and 450cm) a year. That is a lot of rain – imagine the height of your school and multiply that by two, and it probably won't be enough to measure the amount of rain falling in a rainforest per year. These vast areas occupy approximately 6% of the earth's (Q2)...................... and are home to at least half of the earth's plants and animals (Q3).........................

There are two main types of rainforests; tropical and temperate rainforests. The difference between them is that tropical rainforests are very (Q4).................., but they are also wet, and are to be found near the (Q5) .... all around the world. On the other hand, (Q6)............................rainforests are found in cooler parts of the world which also have a high rainfall.

These forests are home for a vast number of species and a variety of colours, shapes and sizes of their inhabitants. The huge towering forest trees provide (Q7)........................ that are perfect for exotic birds, monkeys, and on the ground would be found deadly predators, like lions, prowling through the (Q8)........................... Many people also live in and on the edge of rainforests but despite its huge importance to our lives, rainforests are under threat and many rainforest species are becoming (Q9)............................. Perhaps the biggest threat is (Q10).......................................; or man's need to clear the forests to use for timber.

CONTINUE WORKING

Read the passage and select the most appropriate word from the table below.

A	B	C	D	E
supernatural	existed	lesson	preserved	cultures

F	G	H	I	J
century	versions	sword	generations	miracles

Myths and Legends

Myths and Legends are the traditional or cultural stories of people that were passed on by word of mouth, from one individual to another. They were also passed on from individuals onto groups; a practice that has taken place over many (Q11)...................... These stories have a special significance to the country or culture of the people to whom it belongs. The oral tales were (Q12) .... orally, at a time when books and printing was not available, and when people could not read or write. Some tales have religious figures or (Q13) .... folklore charactes, which reflect beliefs and understanding about the world in general. Whether they are referred to as folk tales, myths or legends, they are all popular stories, some of which survive today in different countries; with various (Q14)...................... of the same story in different (Q15).......................... For example, an African folktale about a spider called *Anansi* (a God in West Africa), is *Brer Anancy,* (a trickster spider in the Caribbean); very different characteristics!

There are differences between myths and legends: Legends are stories which are believed both by tellers and listeners, to have taken place and are thought to be based on historic events. These tales are known to involve heroic characters and may include (Q16) ...., or may change slightly with re-telling over a period of time. For example, the legend of King Arthur is thought to have (Q17).........................between the 5th and 6th (Q18) .... and even today is questioned by those who doubt that he became a Royal person, by just pulling a (Q19) ....from an anvil! On the other hand, Myths are stories that come from traditions or legends, which have a deep symbolic meaning to those who hear and tell it. They are not necessarily the recording of a true event. What is obvious, it usually provides a (Q20)............................ to the hearer or reader. An example of such a myth is the Ancient Greek story of Theseus and the Minotaur. This myth presents fantasy via a monster with horns in the head of a bull and the body of a man. Although there is no real evidence that Theseus existed, it holds symbolism for the reader/hearer of the tale.

STOP AND WAIT FOR FURTHER INSTRUCTIONS

Answer Sheet – Paper 2

COMPREHENSION

	A	B	C	D	E
1	A	B	C	D	E
2	A	B	C	D	E
3	A	B	C	D	E
4	A	B	C	D	E
5	A	B	C	D	E
6	A	B	C	D	E
7	A	B	C	D	E
8	A	B	C	D	E
9	A	B	C	D	E
10	A	B	C	D	E

SYNONYMS Continued

	A	B	C	D	E
10	A	B	C	D	E
11	A	B	C	D	E
12	A	B	C	D	E
13	A	B	C	D	E
14	A	B	C	D	E
15	A	B	C	D	E
16	A	B	C	D	E
17	A	B	C	D	E
18	A	B	C	D	E
19	A	B	C	D	E

SYNONYMS Continued

	A	B	C	D	E
20	A	B	C	D	E
21	A	B	C	D	E
22	A	B	C	D	E
23	A	B	C	D	E
24	A	B	C	D	E

GRAMMAR

	A	B	C	D	E
1	A	B	C	D	E
2	A	B	C	D	E
3	A	B	C	D	E
4	A	B	C	D	E
5	A	B	C	D	E
6	A	B	C	D	E
7	A	B	C	D	E
8	A	B	C	D	E

SHUFFLED SENTENCES

	A	B	C	D	E
1	A	B	C	D	E
2	A	B	C	D	E
3	A	B	C	D	E
4	A	B	C	D	E
5	A	B	C	D	E
6	A	B	C	D	E
7	A	B	C	D	E
8	A	B	C	D	E
9	A	B	C	D	E
10	A	B	C	D	E
11	A	B	C	D	E
12	A	B	C	D	E
13	A	B	C	D	E
14	A	B	C	D	E
15	A	B	C	D	E

ANTONYMS

	A	B	C	D	E
1	A	B	C	D	E
2	A	B	C	D	E
3	A	B	C	D	E
4	A	B	C	D	E
5	A	B	C	D	E
6	A	B	C	D	E
7	A	B	C	D	E
8	A	B	C	D	E
9	A	B	C	D	E
10	A	B	C	D	E
11	A	B	C	D	E
12	A	B	C	D	E
13	A	B	C	D	E
14	A	B	C	D	E
15	A	B	C	D	E

CLOZE – you will need to choose from these LETTERS: A B C D E F G H I J

1				16		
2				17		
3				18		
4				19		
5				20		
6						
7						
8						
9						
10						
11						
12						
13						
14						
15						

SYNONYMS

	A	B	C	D	E
1	A	B	C	D	E
2	A	B	C	D	E
3	A	B	C	D	E
4	A	B	C	D	E
5	A	B	C	D	E
6	A	B	C	D	E
7	A	B	C	D	E
8	A	B	C	D	E
9	A	B	C	D	E

Shade the correct answer box
If the answer is **D** then shade **D**:

Example:

A	B	C	**D**

Test Paper 3

Instructions:

1. Make sure you have pencils and an eraser for this test.
2. You must be able to see a clock or watch.
3. Write your name on the answer sheet.
4. Do not open the question booklet until you are told to do so by the audio instructions.
5. You must listen carefully to the audio instructions given.
6. Mark your answers on the answer sheet only.
7. All workings must be completed on a separate piece of paper.
8. Do not use a calculator, dictionary or thesaurus at any time in the test.
9. Be sure you move through the tests as quickly as possible, but with care.
10. Follow the instructions at the foot of each page.
11. Mark your answers with a horizontal strike, as shown on the answer sheet.
12. If you want to change your answer make sure you rub out your first answer and that your second answer is clearly visible.
13. You can go back and review any questions that are within the section you are working on only.
14. You must wait for further instructions before you move on to another question.

SYMBOLS AND PHRASES USED IN THE TESTS

   Instructions

   Time allowed for this section

   Stop and wait for further instructions

   Continue working

Comprehension

 **INSTRUCTIONS**

 **YOU HAVE 9 MINUTES TO COMPLETE THE FOLLOWING SECTION**

YOU HAVE 10 QUESTIONS TO COMPLETE WITHIN THE TIME GIVEN.

EXAMPLE

Comprehension Example

Before the dreadful accident, the train with its torn seats had rusty window frames and a multitude of spots of chewing gum which covered its worn-out floors. Now looking at the mangled wreck, passengers, who complained about the strange metallic smell, were lucky to have escaped with no injuries.

Example 1

According to the passage, what seems to have had happened to the train?

A   It was dirty
B   It was unpleasant to ride in
C   It was involved in an accident
D   It was scrapped as it was old

The correct answer is C.

STOP AND WAIT FOR FURTHER INSTRUCTIONS

The River Thames

One of the most remarkable features in the City of London is the River Thames. It is the longest river in England, beginning from its source near the village of Kemble in the Cotswolds and snaking its way through Oxford, Reading, Maidenhead, Eton and then Windsor, to the city of London into the sea. It is possible to see some **famous** views as it passes: Syon House, Hampton Court Palace, Richmond, with the famous view of the Thames from Richmond Hill and Kew. Within the City of London, the Thames passes through Greenwich and Dartford before it enters the sea in an estuary called The Nore.

The river is about 346 kilometres long and it is said that London was made capital of Roman Britain at the spot where the tides reached in 43AD. The Romans called the river *Thamesis* and it was an important way to travel between London and Westminster in the 16th and 17th centuries. The river actually froze over in winter during the 17th and 18th century and this led to the first *"Frost Fair"* in 1607, with a tent city erected on the river with lots of amusements, such as ice bowling. The last time the river froze was in 1814. It is believed that the building of a new London Bridge in 1825, which had less pillars than the previous old bridge, made the water flow easier than before. Th previous slow moving water was one of the reasons why the river used to freeze in cold winters.

During the 18th century, the Thames was one of the world's busiest waterways, as London was then the centre of big business during the time of the British Empire. However, it has not always been plain sailing; one of the worst river disasters in England on the Thames was in 1878, when a crowded pleasure boat, *Princess Alice,* crashed into the Bywell Castle, killing over 640people. A more recent disaster took place on 20 August 1989, when a pleasure steamer *Marchioness* sank after being hit twice by the dredger, Bowbelle. The *Marchioness* sank within 20 seconds, killing 51 out of the 79 people on board. Today, with the end of the Empire, and the existence of rail and road transport, the river is less important as a means of business transport than it was before. One visible key feature on the river today is the Thames Barrier which was constructed in the 1980s, to control flooding of London City and to stop water damage to low lying areas up the river in London.

Many tourists visiting London take pictures of the iconic river across the many bridges and tunnel that cross the River Thames. These include Tower Bidge, London Bridge, Lambeth Bridge and Dartford Crossing. The Thames is perhaps one of the most admired rivers in the world and poets, like Roselle Thompson, have praised the iconic feature in *Ode to the Thames* (2019)*. There are also some interesting uses of the Thames during the year. For example, the children's writer and comedian David Walliams, swam the entire length of the 140 mile river in 2011, and raised over £1million for charity. On the annual *Red Nose Day,* many people also swim the Thames for charity. Today, the Thames River bank has become the most magical place to be, as the venue for annual, spectacular firework displays and celebrations, as the nation rings in the New Year in London, every year.

Glossary * *Ode to the Thames* in Rythms of Life: An Anthology of Modern Poetry (2019) Eagle Publications, London.

CONTINUE WORKING

Questions

1. According to *paragraph 1*, at least how many famous sites can you view as the River Thames courses from its source to London City?

   a. There are 4 sites
   b. There are 8 sites
   c. There are 5 sites
   d. There are 7 sites

2. From where does the River Thames begin its journey?
   a. Cotswold
   b. Reading
   c. Oxford
   d. Maidenhead

3. During which period of time was London made capital of Roman Britain?
   a. 16th century
   b. 43AD
   c. 1878
   d. 17th and 18th century

4. Which event took place for the first time on the River in 1607?
   a. Ice skating
   b. A boat race
   c. Camping on ice
   d. A Frost Fair

5. What stopped the Thames River from freezing after 1825?
   a. Lots of fish were found
   b. Less pillars in the water from bridges
   c. The ice cracked causing it to melt
   d. The water in the river became warm

6. According to the passage, name two river disasters on the Thames. **Circle 2**
   a. The British Empire failure
   b. The Marchioness disaster
   c. A Boat race crash on the river
   d. The Princess Alice crash

7. Why is the Thames River used less than it used to be? **Circle 2 correct answers.**
   a. There is less use with the end of the British Empire
   b. Using the Thames could cause more river crashes
   c. Because the water in the Thames is drying up
   d. There is now more use of road and rail for transport

8. From this passage what is the total number of people who dies from disasters on the Thames?
   a. Over 700 people
   b. Less than 500 people
   c. Approximately 650
   d. Around 691 people

CONTINUE WORKING

9. What benefit is the Thames Barrier to London? **Circle at least 2**.
    a. It stops sea creatures from invading London
    b. It prevents flooding across London's low lying areas
    c. It stops the sea from flooding the City
    d. It prevents harmful pollution from reaching the sea

10. Facts about the River Thames – Circle the statements that are **NOT TRUE**
    a. Most people are scared that the Thames will flood London
    b. People swim in the River Thames to raise money for Charity
    c. The Thames River has been praised in a poem
    d. People refuse to go on the River Thames in case of accidents
    e. On New Years Eve each year its one of the favourite places to be

STOP AND WAIT FOR FURTHER INSTRUCTIONS

Shuffled Sentences

# INSTRUCTIONS

YOU HAVE 8 MINUTES TO COMPLETE THE FOLLOWING SECTION

YOU HAVE 15 QUESTIONS TO COMPLETE WITHIN THE TIME GIVEN.

EXAMPLES

Example 1

The following sentence is shuffled and also contains one unnecessary word. Rearrange the sentence correctly in order to identify the unnecessary word.

Train did time on arrive is not the ran.

A	B	C	D	E
work	ran	morning	try	office

The correct answer is B.

Example 2

Someone door the waited the rang for they to farm open bell and

A	B	C	D	E
home	stood	closed	farm	inside

The correct answer is D.

STOP AND WAIT FOR FURTHER INSTRUCTIONS

Shuffled Sentences

These sentences are shuffled and also contain one unnecessary word. Rearrange them correctly in order to identify the word that's unnecessary.

1. Vet the Patrick weekend Ben his took dog the to

A	B	C	D	E
Ben	his	the	took	weekend

2. With a made the play cardboard children with

A	B	C	D	E
made	the	play	with	a

3. Jam the bread caused road a accident fatal road

A	B	C	D	E
jam	a	the	bread	fatal

4. Pool weekend the took swimming an us hour mum to for

A	B	C	D	E
us	weekend	to	for	the

5. All we in garden sausages had we a after the barbecue leaves garden swept

A	B	C	D	E
in	had	leaves	a	sausages

6. At local fence our weekend a the garden built Saturday builder

A	B	C	D	E
Saturday	the	built	local	a

7. Morning got not detention for homework his yesterday doing Tom

A	B	C	D	E
not	doing	for	morning	his

8. Hamburger loves drink in food hates Derek in gerkhin but

A	B	C	D	E
in	drink	food	but	loves

CONTINUE WORKING

9. Lessons day in fell during heavily all break-time stayed we the rain so

A	B	C	D	E
fell	in	lessons	we	the

10. Last fire called shopping firemen put centre out a were to at the

A	B	C	D	E
put	last	out	at	were

11. Tourists visit Palace summer the London months many during

A	B	C	D	E
Palace	the	many	months	during

12. Time bike ride boy a struggled hill his up the to

A	B	C	D	E
a	up	to	time	his

13. Weekend with camping school the children their went

A	B	C	D	E
the	their	with	weekend	went

14. Read Monday end promised of book the end Jack week to his new before

A	B	C	D	E
read	end	Monday	his	to

15. Arrive soon game they with waited to PS4 for the postman new their

A	B	C	D	E
new	they	the	to	soon

STOP AND WAIT FOR FURTHER INSTRUCTIONS

Synonyms

 **INSTRUCTIONS**

 YOU HAVE **7** MINUTES TO COMPLETE THE FOLLOWING SECTION

YOU HAVE **24** QUESTIONS TO COMPLETE WITHIN THE TIME GIVEN.

EXAMPLES

Example 1

Select the word that is most similar in meaning to the following word:

tranquil

A	B	C	D	E
rowdy	windy	quite	peaceful	reach

The correct answer is D.

Example 2

Select the word that is most similar in meaning to the following word:

humorous

A	B	C	D	E
humble	peculiar	holy	comic	creative

The correct answer is C.

STOP AND WAIT FOR FURTHER INSTRUCTIONS

Synonyms

There are 24 questions to complete in this time. You have 7 minutes to complete this section.

Select the word from the table that is most similar in meaning to the word above the table.

1. ASSIST

A	B	C	D	E
close	try	help	ordinary	pleased

2. ARTIFICIAL

A	B	C	D	E
fake	honest	beside	art	creative

3. SUSPEND

A	B	C	D	E
suspicious	sincere	hang	sudden	deserve

4. IDLE

A	B	C	D	E
isolate	impolite	haste	shy	inactive

5. GRADIENT

A	B	C	D	E
slender	slope	slow	treat	courage

6. REMOTE

A	B	C	D	E
depress	near	distant	favour	exhausted

7. DISPLAY

A	B	C	D	E
disturb	show	develop	drab	playful

8. MEAGRE

A	B	C	D	E
more	massive	temper	scanty	trouble

9. CALAMITY

A	B	C	D	E
merry	peace	public	closure	disaster

CONTINUE WORKING

10. GUARD

A	B	C	D	E
protect	practice	locket	guarantee	gasp

11. HEROIC

A	B	C	D	E
brave	pretend	measure	handsome	hopeful

12. GROPE

A	B	C	D	E
false	feel	greedy	perceive	personal

13. AFFECTIONATE

A	B	C	D	E
hate	effective	irritate	loving	punish

14. LOFTY

A	B	C	D	E
snobbish	dismiss	high	roof	packaging

15. COMPREHEND

A	B	C	D	E
compose	complicated	understand	frighten	maintain

16. FOE

A	B	C	D	E
clarity	enemy	feasible	fool	scold

17. TRICK

A	B	C	D	E
			deceive	

18. TWILIGHT

A	B	C	D	E
twice	dusk	trespass	lighten	activity

19. ASSEMBLE

A	B	C	D	E
gather				

CONTINUE WORKING

20. ATTIRE

A	B	C	D	E
attitude	clothes	hint	altitude	avoid

21. PROFIT

A	B	C	D	E
intention	provide	gain	capture	pronounce

22. SUFFICIENT

A	B	C	D	E
ignore	distant	enough	suffer	stressful

23. COAX

A	B	C	D	E
shout	persuade	practice	struggle	corner

24. DISPERSE

A	B	C	D	E
displease	captive	escape	throw	scatter

STOP AND WAIT FOR FURTHER INSTRUCTIONS

Grammar

⚠ INSTRUCTIONS

YOU HAVE 5 MINUTES TO COMPLETE THE FOLLOWING SECTION

YOU HAVE 8 QUESTIONS TO COMPLETE WITHIN THE TIME GIVEN.

EXAMPLES

Example 1 - Select the word from the boxes below that is misspelt

A	B	C	D	E
lifes	open	sweet	repeat	bishop

The correct answer is A.

Example 2 - Select the correct prefix or suffix below to give the opposite to the word *mature.*

A	B	C	D	E
in	il	im	re	non

The correct answer is C.

STOP AND WAIT FOR FURTHER INSTRUCTIONS

1. Select a **simile** for the word **"snail"** from the words below.

A	B	C	D	E
real	rapid	fast	slow	long

2. Select the **homophone** for the word **"grown"** from the words below.

A	B	C	D	E
known	groan	loan	support	male

3. Identify the **antonym** for the word **"barren"**.

A	B	C	D	E
leaking	barrel	gamble	fertile	metal

4. Select the word that is **misspelt**.

A	B	C	D	E
generousity	confine	wary	spectacles	entice

5. Identify the **homonym** of the word **"wholly."**

A	B	C	D	E
folly	slowly	holy	gain	possible

6. Identify the **Antonym** for the word **"ascend."**

A	B	C	D	E
descend	altitude	displease	disturb	distant

7. Identify the **possessive pronoun** from the words below.

A	B	C	D	E
them	theirs	we	he	they

8. Identify the **synonym** of the word **"wretched"**.

A	B	C	D	E
upbeat	bored	loud	miserable	complain

STOP AND WAIT FOR FURTHER INSTRUCTIONS

Antonyms

 **INSTRUCTIONS**

 YOU HAVE **5** MINUTES TO COMPLETE THE FOLLOWING SECTION

YOU HAVE **15** QUESTIONS TO COMPLETE WITHIN THE TIME GIVEN.

EXAMPLES

Example 1

Which word is least similar to the following word:

dark

A	B	C	D	E
night	morning	light	bright	heavy

The correct answer is C.

Example 2

Which word is least similar to the following word:

departure

A	B	C	D	E
entrance	main	rough	arrival	below

The correct answer is D.

STOP AND WAIT FOR FURTHER INSTRUCTIONS

Choose a word from each box below, that is opposite to the word in the question:

1. *timid*

A	B	C	D	E
tired	bold	energetic	happy	cross

2. *inferior*

A	B	C	D	E
gain	interior	quarrel	stern	superior

3. *fail*

A	B	C	D	E
pass	supply	satisfied	cry	unhappy

4. *shallow*

A	B	C	D	E
determine	shout	deep	shadow	sauce

5. *defeat*

A	B	C	D	E
detected	distress	quiet	win	determined

6. *guilty*

A	B	C	D	E
innocent	calm	confident	respected	lie

7. *sober*

A	B	C	D	E
stern	crying	drunk	display	remote

8. *stale*

A	B	C	D	E
stalling	stable	peculiar	frosty	fresh

CONTINUE WORKING

9. tame

A	B	C	D	E
touchy	trespass	wild	windy	terror

10. wax

A	B	C	D	E
watery	candle	wane	fire	run

11. refuse

A	B	C	D	E
	accept			

12. senior

A	B	C	D	E
superior	stable	satisfy	justice	junior

13. freedom

A	B	C	D	E
frighten	fragrant	captive	favourite	free

14. minority

A	B	C	D	E
minors	mute	majority	minutes	monstrous

15. employee

A	B	C	D	E
employer	empathise	entertainment	favourite	loyal

STOP AND WAIT FOR FURTHER INSTRUCTIONS

Cloze

⚠ INSTRUCTIONS

🕐 YOU HAVE **10** MINUTES TO COMPLETE THE FOLLOWING SECTION

YOU HAVE **20** QUESTIONS TO COMPLETE WITHIN THE TIME GIVEN.

EXAMPLES

Example 1

Read the sentence below and select the most appropriate word from the table.

A	B	C	D	E
canopy	canvas	scenery	display	picture

The wall of the abandoned building was the perfect ………………………….for the painter.

Example 2

Read the sentence below and select the most appropriate word from the table.

A	B	C	D	E
send	call	attend	reply	absent

We are expected to …………………..to the wedding invitation before the end of the month.

STOP AND WAIT FOR FURTHER INSTRUCTIONS

Read the passage and select the most appropriate word from the table below.

A	B	C	D	E
million	climate	bitter	darker	mass

F	G	H	I	J
ingredient	matured	globe	world	nutritional

Where does your favourite chocolate come from?

Did you know that chocolate is grown on a tree? Yes, the favourite of millions of people around the (Q1) ...., began 100 (Q2) ....years ago. Chocolate is actually made from cocoa beans, grown on trees that are found in South and Central America, Africa and the Caribbean. In fact, 70% of the cocoa grown in the (Q3) .... comes from Africa.

It takes roughly 3 to 4 years for a tree to be fully (Q4) ....and they like growing in both hot and rainy (Q5)........................ Just imagine, one cocoa tree can produce up to 2000 pods which grow on branches and each pod contains between 30 to 40 seeds inside. These seeds are called beans and it's the main (Q6) ....in chocolate.

When the seeds are dried in the sun and roasted and cleaned, they can be pounded, ground, pressed, or heated; until they become a very soft, dark brown, (Q7)............................ This is the natural cocoa, which is (Q8) .... to taste. It is also very (Q9) ...., containing high levels of Vitamin C, magnesium and some caffeine. The more cocoa mass in the chocolate, the (Q10)...........................the colour – that's why plain chocolate is dark as it does not have milk in it. It is the milk ingredients and sweetner that make the chocolate lighter in colour and creamier to taste.

CONTINUE WORKING

Read the passage and select the most appropriate word from the table below.

A	B	C	D	E
clasped	nudge	disbelief	stiffly	alerted

F	G	H	I	J
siblings	shrugged	neighbourhod	tiptoed	suspicious

The Burglary

The bright, yellow stars in the dark night twinkled in the sky, as I turned from reading my book to gaze at them. This would be a good time to take a short break, to ease my tired eyes from the strain of reading non-stop for the past two hours. My twin brothers and I had gone up to bed as usual at 9pm, but it wasn't long before my (Q11)....................... had fallen asleep. There was peace at last and my book; heaven, I thought!

Suddenly there was a noise from downstairs and this (Q12)....................... me. I froze. I tried waking up my siblings with a hard (Q13)........................., trying not to speak, in case I could be heard but they just kept on turning the other way and continued sleeping. Things were not as they should be, I thought.

However, after a while, all was quiet and I (Q14)............................. off my earlier fears, thinking I was nervous and panicky for nothing. Nevertheless, I was nosey and wanted to make sure all was well. I took my umbrella and (Q15)...........................onto the landing, listening as I did so. Then down the wooden stairs, I wasked softly and carefully, so as not wake anyone or I wont hear the last of it in the morning. I tip-toed then reached downstairs.

Surprisingly, there was some soft whispering and a shadow moved quickly, sharply, against the wall. I stood (Q16)........................... breathing deeply, trying not to let them see me. Then another shadow moved across the kitchen into the living room, where he met the first shadow. They were going through drawers with a torch and I was horrified. Robbers! I had to tell someone, anyone, but one clumsy step alerted the men that someone was watching them. When they turned around, they shone their torch straight into my eyes. One of them grabbed me from behind and (Q17)..................... his huge, gloved hand over my mouth. I was unable to scream, move or call out. I tried to wriggle to loosen myself but he was too strong.

Then he picked me up as easy as a rag doll and I let my umbrella dropped on to a pot, to deliberately make a noise. Instantly, voices were heard upstairs with movements then lights flicked on. My parents were (Q18)...........................and thankfully, they were walking on the landing and slowly moving down the stairs. The two men looked at each other in (Q19).............................and instantly let me go and made a run for it with what little they had found. I cowered in the corner in shock, until my parents found me. Hearing what I had to say, they instantly called the police. It appeared that a number of people in our (Q20)............................ had had their jewellery stolen in the past 10 days. Luckily, they had mistakenly run off with our fake gold and silver; since our real jewellery was kept locked in a bank's vault.

STOP AND WAIT FOR FURTHER INSTRUCTIONS

Answer Sheet – Paper 3

COMPREHENSION

1	A	B	C	D	E
2	A	B	C	D	E
3	A	B	C	D	E
4	A	B	C	D	E
5	A	B	C	D	E
6	A	B	C	D	E
7	A	B	C	D	E
8	A	B	C	D	E
9	A	B	C	D	E
10	A	B	C	D	E

SYNONYMS Continued

10	A	B	C	D	E
11	A	B	C	D	E
12	A	B	C	D	E
13	A	B	C	D	E
14	A	B	C	D	E
15	A	B	C	D	E
16	A	B	C	D	E
17	A	B	C	D	E
18	A	B	C	D	E
19	A	B	C	D	E

SYNONYMS Continued

20	A	B	C	D	E
21	A	B	C	D	E
22	A	B	C	D	E
23	A	B	C	D	E
24	A	B	C	D	E

GRAMMAR

1	A	B	C	D	E
2	A	B	C	D	E
3	A	B	C	D	E
4	A	B	C	D	E
5	A	B	C	D	E
6	A	B	C	D	E
7	A	B	C	D	E
8	A	B	C	D	E

SHUFFLED SENTENCES

1	A	B	C	D	E
2	A	B	C	D	E
3	A	B	C	D	E
4	A	B	C	D	E
5	A	B	C	D	E
6	A	B	C	D	E
7	A	B	C	D	E
8	A	B	C	D	E
9	A	B	C	D	E
10	A	B	C	D	E
11	A	B	C	D	E
12	A	B	C	D	E
13	A	B	C	D	E
14	A	B	C	D	E
15	A	B	C	D	E

ANTONYMS

1	A	B	C	D	E
2	A	B	C	D	E
3	A	B	C	D	E
4	A	B	C	D	E
5	A	B	C	D	E
6	A	B	C	D	E
7	A	B	C	D	E
8	A	B	C	D	E
9	A	B	C	D	E
10	A	B	C	D	E
11	A	B	C	D	E
12	A	B	C	D	E
13	A	B	C	D	E
14	A	B	C	D	E
15	A	B	C	D	E

CLOZE – you will need to choose from these LETTERS: A B C D E F G H I J

1					
2					
3					
4					
5					
6					
7					
8					
9					
10					
11					
12					
13					
14					
15					
16					
17					
18					
19					
20					

SYNONYMS

1	A	B	C	D	E
2	A	B	C	D	E
3	A	B	C	D	E
4	A	B	C	D	E
5	A	B	C	D	E
6	A	B	C	D	E
7	A	B	C	D	E
8	A	B	C	D	E
9	A	B	C	D	E

Shade the correct answer box
If the answer is D then shade D:

Example:

A	B	C	D

Test Paper 4

Instructions:

1. Make sure you have pencils and an eraser for this test.
2. You must be able to see a clock or watch.
3. Write your name on the answer sheet.
4. Do not open the question booklet until you are told to do so by the audio instructions.
5. You must listen carefully to the audio instructions given.
6. Mark your answers on the answer sheet only.
7. All workings must be completed on a separate piece of paper.
8. Do not use a calculator, dictionary or thesaurus at any time in the test.
9. Be sure you move through the tests as quickly as possible, but with care.
10. Follow the instructions at the foot of each page.
11. Mark your answers with a horizontal strike, as shown on the answer sheet.
12. If you want to change your answer make sure you rub out your first answer and that your second answer is clearly visible.
13. You can go back and review any questions that are within the section you are working on only.
14. You must wait for further instructions before you move on to another question.

SYMBOLS AND PHRASES USED IN THE TESTS

 Instructions

 Time allowed for this section

 Stop and wait for further instructions

 Continue working

Comprehension

INSTRUCTIONS

YOU HAVE 9 MINUTES TO COMPLETE THE FOLLOWING SECTION

YOU HAVE 10 QUESTIONS TO COMPLETE WITHIN THE TIME GIVEN.

EXAMPLE

Comprehension Example

Before the dreadful accident, the train with its torn seats had rusty window frames and a multitude of spots of chewing gum which covered its worn-out floors. Now looking at the mangled wreck, passengers, who complained about the strange metallic smell, were lucky to have escaped with no injuries.

Example 1

According to the passage, what seems to have had happened to the train?

A It was dirty
B It was unpleasant to ride in
C It was involved in an accident
D It was scrapped as it was old

The correct answer is C.

STOP AND WAIT FOR FURTHER INSTRUCTIONS

LETTING GO

1 She defied the children's *PGL school-trip rule,
   Turning up at 11 am outside of our school;
   Then unsettled the earlier fragile, weepy ones
   Who said goodbyes, and now expectant of fun.

5 They filed out in twos, clutching their little bags,
   Fully coated and each sporting school name-tags;
   Excited though hushed, they followed Miss' lead
   To wait for the coach that's all they now need.

   But mum stood on the opposite pavement
10 Waving, blowing kisses; those were well-meant,
   Whilst silently mouthing, "*Love you my darling,*"
   Knowing I could get into trouble for calling.

   Closer outside my window she stood in the road,
   She tapped on the glass and to me she showed,
15 My battered, one-eyed, and very worn-out Ted,
   A sleeping partner, who never ever leaves my bed.

   I gasped in surprise and felt quite, quite ashamed,
   Of others knowing I still have a teddy with a name;
   Embarrassed, I cringed and slid onto the coach floor
20 And wished I could bolt out the coach entry door.

   My friends, they all laughed, "*You still have a teddy?*"
   "*Course not,*" I blushed; my face red like a cherry,
   I secretly wished the coach would start up and leave;
   My head's in a spin, and my stomach's about to heave.

25 *"Go home mum; stop ruining my growing street **cred;
   I no longer want a teddy anywhere near to my bed!"*
   I did let him go only last night when finally I realized
   Boys like me are more grown up and also quite wise.

By Roselle Thompson

Glossary:
***PGL** is a residential holiday destination for children 7 to 17yrs, a type of summer-camp away from parents.
****cred** – short for *credibility* or street reputation among friends
"*Letting Go*" in **Rythms of Life: An Anthology of Modern Verse** (2019); Eagle Publications

CONTINUE WORKING

Questions

1. Where is the child when the events are taking place in this poem?
   a. On a bike
   b. In a school bus
   c. In a car
   d. In a coach

2. What information about the children is given in *Verse 2*?
   a. They are excited to go away
   b. They have been crying
   c. They were told off by their teacher
   d. They are in an assembly

3. What time of the day is the event taking place?
   a. In the middle of the day
   b. As soon as the children arrive at school
   c. At 11 am, after they arrive at school
   d. After the children's lunch time

4. What *adjective* best describes the child's mother?
   a. Worried and anxious
   b. Excited and loving
   c. Peaceful and calm
   d. Frightened and quiet

5. Why did the child's mother knock on the coach window?
   a. To show him his bag which he had forgotten
   b. She wanted to kiss him goodbye
   c. Her son had forgotten his favourite toy
   d. He had forgotten his school lunch

6. Where was the mother standing in the poem?
   a. In front of the coach
   b. Next to the entrance door of the coach
   c. Opposite to where the coach was
   d. She was standing behind the coach

CONTINUE WORKING

7. Which word best describes the child in *Line 24*?
   a. Excited
   b. Anxious
   c. Alone
   d. Embarassed

8. What did the child feel like doing?
   a. Calling out to his mother
   b. Waving back to her
   c. Hiding from his mother
   d. Running out of the coach

9. How do the listeners on the coach react in *Line 21*?
   a. They laughed at the boy
   b. They called out to the child's mum
   c. They opened the coach door for her
   d. They are angry that she is there

10. Look at *lines 25 and 26*, how does the child feel about the situation?
    a. He is happy to see his mother and waves at her
    b. He feels ashamed and wishes mum would stop embarassing him
    c. He laughs with his friends and ignores his mum
    d. He wants his mum to keep the teddy by his bed until he returns

STOP AND WAIT FOR FURTHER INSTRUCTIONS

Shuffled Sentences

 INSTRUCTIONS

 YOU HAVE **8** MINUTES TO COMPLETE THE FOLLOWING SECTION

YOU HAVE **15** QUESTIONS TO COMPLETE WITHIN THE TIME GIVEN.

EXAMPLES

Example 1

The following sentence is shuffled and also contains one unnecessary word. Rearrange the sentence correctly in order to identify the unnecessary word.

Train did time on arrive is not the ran.

A	B	C	D	E
work	ran	morning	try	office

The correct answer is B.

Example 2

Someone door the waited the rang for they to farm open bell and

A	B	C	D	E
home	stood	closed	farm	inside

The correct answer is D.

STOP AND WAIT FOR FURTHER INSTRUCTIONS

Shuffled Sentences

These sentences are shuffled and also contain one unnecessary word. Rearrange them correctly in order to identify the word that's unnecessary.

1. Pool in played their children all long swimming day the

A	B	C	D	E
long	of	his	the	in

2. Stick dog our in of buried the bone his garden the corner

A	B	C	D	E
her	nervous	stick	was	today

3. Took when morning was test nervous her today she

A	B	C	D	E
test	took	morning	was	she

4. Train us dad London Zoo the new took pandas at us to

A	B	C	D	E
all	train	new	the	us

5. Ran into all we of out went class off alarm the fire when the

A	B	C	D	E
of	out	clas	into	when

6. Fast trains cancelled to bad London weather were all trains

A	B	C	D	E
to	were	all	we	fast

7. Printer yesterday new black she ink needs her for

A	B	C	D	E
yesterday	she	for	her	new

8. Farmer animals him we milk visited gave cheese us extra and when the

A	B	C	D	E
we	and	when	the	animals

CONTINUE WORKING

9. Today any there time a see lot Madam Tussauds see time

A	B	C	D	E
a	time	today	see	there

10. Uncooked not is meat it which is unsafe eat to

A	B	C	D	E
not	is	it	unsafe	to

11. Tigers science wildlife in plenty studied we of interesting

A	B	C	D	E
plenty	of	we	tigers	in

12. Scientists the future believe increasing earth is temperature of the

A	B	C	D	E
is	future	of	the	believe

13. She carry her borrow gloves to prefers than wear them rather

A	B	C	D	E
her	to	borrow	them	than

14. Wedding costume opportunity great event up great to dress

A	B	C	D	E
up	to	great	costume	dress

15. Reason her permission out go to parents gave her

A	B	C	D	E
to	reason	her	gave	go

STOP AND WAIT FOR FURTHER INSTRUCTIONS

Synonyms

 **INSTRUCTIONS**

 YOU HAVE **7** MINUTES TO COMPLETE THE FOLLOWING SECTION

YOU HAVE **24** QUESTIONS TO COMPLETE WITHIN THE TIME GIVEN.

EXAMPLES

Example 1

Select the word that is most similar in meaning to the following word:

tranquil

A	B	C	D	E
rowdy	windy	quite	peaceful	reach

The correct answer is D.

Example 2

Select the word that is most similar in meaning to the following word:

humorous

A	B	C	D	E
humble	peculiar	holy	comic	creative

The correct answer is C.

STOP AND WAIT FOR FURTHER INSTRUCTIONS

Synonyms

There are 24 questions to complete in this time. You have 7 minutes to complete this section.

Select the word from the table that is most similar in meaning to the word above the table.

1. **FABRICATE**

A	B	C	D	E
communicate	tried	lie	reply	shower

2. **INITIATE**

A	B	C	D	E
silent	start	individual	innocent	beauty

3. **SIZEABLE**

A	B	C	D	E
hide	middle	huge	exclude	interior

4. **OBSOLETE**

A	B	C	D	E
absent	attitude	outdated	obtain	order

5. **COUNTERFEIT**

A	B	C	D	E
follow	original	slender	complete	fake

6. **UNFOUNDED**

A	B	C	D	E
keep	trial	suspect	untrue	underneath

7. **HASTILY**

A	B	C	D	E
happiness	fondly	saunter	hurriedly	gallop

8. **CUSTOMARY**

A	B	C	D	E
custard	usual	completed	confide	forward

CONTINUE WORKING

9. VETERAN

A	B	C	D	E
reward	viper	victory	disturb	experienced

10. SUBSTANTIAL

A	B	C	D	E
large	substance	constant	ignorance	repeated

11. HAZARDOUS

A	B	C	D	E
sustain	wondrous	unsafe	relate	trouble

12. REPULSIVE

A	B	C	D	E
ugly	restrictive	reply	wrath	commit

13. GALLANT

A	B	C	D	E
gallop	gratitude	brave	fragrant	insincere

14. INFAMOUS

A	B	C	D	E
notorious	repetitive	reasonable	detain	newspaper

15. ELABORATE

A	B	C	D	E
celebrate	hindrance	topple	wishful	decorative

16. ACCELERATE

A	B	C	D	E
verify	speed	comply	trial	busy

17. ACCOMPLISH

A	B	C	D	E
wish	examine	achieve	coach	determine

CONTINUE WORKING

18. ACQUIRE

A	B	C	D	E
acquaintance	followers	obtain	excite	resume

19. RETAIN

A	B	C	D	E
keep	possibility	refresh	respect	attitude

20. EXPOSE

A	B	C	D	E
expire	exempt	realise	replicate	reveal

21. PLUNGE

A	B	C	D	E
providence	fall	lavish	plaster	protectice

22. RESOLVE

A	B	C	D	E
method	settle	scamper	respect	removal

23. DESIGNATE

A	B	C	D	E
destructive	embassy	choose	cheerful	fiery

24. GATHER

A	B	C	D	E
altitude	refute	accordingly	controversy	acumulate

STOP AND WAIT FOR FURTHER INSTRUCTIONS

Grammar

⚠ INSTRUCTIONS

🕐 YOU HAVE **5** MINUTES TO COMPLETE THE FOLLOWING SECTION

YOU HAVE **8** QUESTIONS TO COMPLETE WITHIN THE TIME GIVEN.

EXAMPLES

Example 1 - Select the word from the boxes below that is *misspelt*

A	B	C	D	E
lifes	open	sweet	repeat	bishop

The correct answer is A.

Example 2 - Select the correct *prefix or suffix* below to give the opposite to the word *mature.*

A	B	C	D	E
in	il	im	re	non

The correct answer is C.

STOP AND WAIT FOR FURTHER INSTRUCTIONS

1. Select the **Past Participle** for the word **"ring"** from the words below.

A	B	C	D	E
rode	rash	rung	repeat	rude

2. Select the **Homophone** for the word **"lightning"** from the words below.

A	B	C	D	E
lighter	listless	lightening	liberty	lastly

3. Identify the **Antonym** for the word **"miserly"**.

A	B	C	D	E
restrain	generous	poorly	general	determine

4. Select the word that is **misspelt**.

A	B	C	D	E
comittee	complaint	meddle	gambol	intrude

5. Identify the **Homonym** of the word **"heir."**

A	B	C	D	E
new	height	fare	air	eight

6. Identify the **Superlative** for the word **"little."**

A	B	C	D	E
patient	lightly	kinder	bigger	least

7. Identify the **Pronoun** from the words below.

A	B	C	D	E
that	therefore	despite	people	things

8. Identify the **Conjunction** from the words below.

A	B	C	D	E
either	leave	it	lastly	similar

STOP AND WAIT FOR FURTHER INSTRUCTIONS

Antonyms

 **INSTRUCTIONS**

 **YOU HAVE 5 MINUTES TO COMPLETE THE FOLLOWING SECTION**

YOU HAVE 15 QUESTIONS TO COMPLETE WITHIN THE TIME GIVEN.

EXAMPLES

Example 1

Which word is least similar to the following word:

dark

A	B	C	D	E
night	morning	light	bright	heavy

The correct answer is C.

Example 2

Which word is least similar to the following word:

departure

A	B	C	D	E
entrance	main	rough	arrival	below

The correct answer is D.

STOP AND WAIT FOR FURTHER INSTRUCTIONS

Choose a word from each box below, that is opposite to the word in the question:

1. accumulate

A	B	C	D	E
accolade	get	gather	triumph	scatter

2. scamper

A	B	C	D	E
stand	solve	forward	interesting	helper

3. vertical

A	B	C	D	E
unit	erect	contemplate	horizontal	care

4. stagnant

A	B	C	D	E
slow	considerate	moving	send	score

5. driver

A	B	C	D	E
wander	continue	contain	passenger	listen

6. host

A	B	C	D	E
examine	trust	kill	exhale	guest

7. solid

A	B	C	D	E
wander	hover	liquid	help	forgive

8. retreat

A	B	C	D	E
slender	cut	nickel	advance	leisure

CONTINUE WORKING

9. war

A	B	C	D	E
peace	fly	confide	summon	search

10. ebb

A	B	C	D	E
better	between	comfort	flow	understand

11. coarse

A	B	C	D	E
proclaim	measure	matter	fine	method

12. bitter

A	B	C	D	E
exit	sweet	thrust	exit	separate

13. bent

A	B	C	D	E
although	forward	adhoc	compromise	straight

14. feeble

A	B	C	D	E
valley	veteran	hide	strong	range

15. prosperity

A	B	C	D	E
suspect	supernatural	poverty	contrast	maintain

STOP AND WAIT FOR FURTHER INSTRUCTIONS

Cloze

 INSTRUCTIONS

 YOU HAVE **10** MINUTES TO COMPLETE THE FOLLOWING SECTION

YOU HAVE **20** QUESTIONS TO COMPLETE WITHIN THE TIME GIVEN.

EXAMPLES

Example 1

Read the sentence below and select the most appropriate word from the table.

A	B	C	D	E
canopy	canvas	scenery	display	picture

The wall of the abandoned building was the perfect ………………………………for the painter.

Example 2

Read the sentence below and select the most appropriate word from the table.

A	B	C	D	E
send	call	attend	reply	absent

We are expected to …………………………to the wedding invitation before the end of the month.

STOP AND WAIT FOR FURTHER INSTRUCTIONS

Read the passage and select the most appropriate word from the table below.

A	B	C	D	E
Europe	inherited	intervened	Baker	bombings

F	G	H	I	J
Royal	attractions	exhibitions	fire	imprisoned

Madam Tussauds

Madam Tussauds is one of the most popular tourists (Q1).................... in London. It displays waxworks of famous and historical figures, as well as popular celebrities, film and television stars and famous actors. This wax museum was founded by Marie Tussaud, a wax sculptor who was born in France. She learnt how to make models from wax from her father since she was six years old. Marie created her first exhibited wax model in 1777, when she was 17 years old. Life was not always easy-going for Marie, as during the French Revolution, she was (Q2)..........................for 3 months and it was planned to execute her. Luckily, a powerful friend (Q3)...................on her behalf and she was set free.

When her father died in 1794, Marie (Q4)...............................his huge collection of wax models, and for 33 years she travelled around (Q5)..........................with her models in a touring show which she called *Madam Tussaud's.* She was invited by well-known figures in London to exhibit her work alongside theirs, at the Lyceum Theatre, but at that time, there was not a lot of money to be made from her (Q6)..........................

However, whilst in London, war broke out and Marie was unable to return to France. She settled down in (Q7).......................Street and opened up a museum, with the famous *Chamber of Horrors* exhibition being her main attraction. This part of her exhibition included victims of the French Revolution, murderrers and criminals. She had a total of 400 different figures but in 1925 (Q8)...........................damaged some of the models. Furthermore, by 1941 with the Second World War, most of her older models were destroyed by (Q9)............................ There are some sculptures which still exist, that Marie Tussaud made herself. For example, in 1842, she made a self-portrait, which is now on display at the entrance of her museum. She died in her sleep on 16th April 1850. Today, her work lives on in over 25 countries around the globe: Asia, Europe, America, and Australia. Visitors are able to admire Madame Tussaud's wax figures, which include historical and (Q10)………………………..figures, film stars, sports stars, and famous murderers.

CONTINUE WORKING

A	B	C	D	E
procedure	transfer	purchases	filling	emitted

F	G	H	I	J
access	transactions	communication	programs	inaccessible

The Internet

Nowadays, almost everyone in the world has come into contact with computers. A great many of them have been using the internet and there are advantages and disadvantages to this. First of all, the internet provides (Q11).....................to a lot of information. Some of them are very useful for jobs; general education and online teaching, as well as marking and setting children school work; medical assistance; desperately needed (Q12)...........................; pre-school and home-school learning as well as help with your hobbies. Searching the net with Google, you can find nearly everything you want. You can also do shopping using the internet, especially for those who are housebound and can't get out because they are sick, frail or unable to walk. Of course, there is a certain kind of pleasure walking into a store and feeling some of the goods you want to buy before you make your (Q13)............................. but if you need something that's (Q14)........................, you may be able to buy it in online shops.

You need only select what you want – the (Q15)......................................nowadays is simple: fill in some forms, and then click **OK**. In some cases, in less than an hour you will get what you ordered delivered directly to your home, without having to leave your computer screen! You can pay with your credit card, pay cash on delivery when you get the package, or (Q16).......................money from your bank account. All banks offer easy transfer of money on the internet. It is faster than going into the bank and (Q17)..........................in forms. Transferring money in traditional ways take a lot longer; using the internet you can do this in a fw seconds, including weekends and any time of day or night! What's more, bank internet (Q18).......................... have some measure of safety with insurance against unauthorized transactions and theft.

The next advantage of the internet is emails. You can get and send mails in a few seconds. The fact is you can pretty much email whatever you want these days; movies, photos, songs, computer (Q19)........................... and books. And what about the cost, it much cheaper than buying a stamp to send a letter through the slow mail (the postman). The internet does have disadvantages though - the length of time spent on the computer, radiation (Q20)..........................by computer screens, harm to your eyes, lack of evercise, and addiction. However, as with everything, it's always sensible to create a balance in your life, as you enjoy, and make great use of this technology.

STOP AND WAIT FOR FURTHER INSTRUCTIONS

Answer Sheet – Paper 4

COMPREHENSION						SYNONYMS Continued						SYNONYMS Continued						GRAMMAR					
1	A	B	C	D	E	10	A	B	C	D	E	20	A	B	C	D	E	1	A	B	C	D	E
2	A	B	C	D	E	11	A	B	C	D	E	21	A	B	C	D	E	2	A	B	C	D	E
3	A	B	C	D	E	12	A	B	C	D	E	22	A	B	C	D	E	3	A	B	C	D	E
4	A	B	C	D	E	13	A	B	C	D	E	23	A	B	C	D	E	4	A	B	C	D	E
5	A	B	C	D	E	14	A	B	C	D	E	24	A	B	C	D	E	5	A	B	C	D	E
6	A	B	C	D	E	15	A	B	C	D	E							6	A	B	C	D	E
7	A	B	C	D	E	16	A	B	C	D	E							7	A	B	C	D	E
8	A	B	C	D	E	17	A	B	C	D	E							8	A	B	C	D	E
9	A	B	C	D	E	18	A	B	C	D	E												
10	A	B	C	D	E	19	A	B	C	D	E												

SHUFFLED SENTENCES						ANTONYMS						CLOZE – you will need to choose from these LETTERS: A B C D E F G H I J											
1	A	B	C	D	E	1	A	B	C	D	E	1						16					
2	A	B	C	D	E	2	A	B	C	D	E	2						17					
3	A	B	C	D	E	3	A	B	C	D	E	3						18					
4	A	B	C	D	E	4	A	B	C	D	E	4						19					
5	A	B	C	D	E	5	A	B	C	D	E	5						20					
6	A	B	C	D	E	6	A	B	C	D	E	6											
7	A	B	C	D	E	7	A	B	C	D	E	7											
8	A	B	C	D	E	8	A	B	C	D	E	8											
9	A	B	C	D	E	9	A	B	C	D	E	9											
10	A	B	C	D	E	10	A	B	C	D	E	10											
11	A	B	C	D	E	11	A	B	C	D	E	11											
12	A	B	C	D	E	12	A	B	C	D	E	12											
13	A	B	C	D	E	13	A	B	C	D	E	13											
14	A	B	C	D	E	14	A	B	C	D	E	14											
15	A	B	C	D	E	15	A	B	C	D	E	15											

SYNONYMS					
1	A	B	C	D	E
2	A	B	C	D	E
3	A	B	C	D	E
4	A	B	C	D	E
5	A	B	C	D	E
6	A	B	C	D	E
7	A	B	C	D	E
8	A	B	C	D	E
9	A	B	C	D	E

Shade the correct answer box
If the answer is **D** then shade **D**:

Example:

A	B	C	**D**

Test Paper 5

Instructions:

1. Make sure you have pencils and an eraser for this test.
2. You must be able to see a clock or watch.
3. Write your name on the answer sheet.
4. Do not open the question booklet until you are told to do so by the audio instructions.
5. You must listen carefully to the audio instructions given.
6. Mark your answers on the answer sheet only.
7. All workings must be completed on a separate piece of paper.
8. Do not use a calculator, dictionary or thesaurus at any time in the test.
9. Be sure you move through the tests as quickly as possible, but with care.
10. Follow the instructions at the foot of each page.
11. Mark your answers with a horizontal strike, as shown on the answer sheet.
12. If you want to change your answer make sure you rub out your first answer and that your second answer is clearly visible.
13. You can go back and review any questions that are within the section you are working on only.
14. You must wait for further instructions before you move on to another question.

SYMBOLS AND PHRASES USED IN THE TESTS

 Instructions

 Time allowed for this section

 Stop and wait for further instructions

 Continue working

Comprehension

 **INSTRUCTIONS**

YOU HAVE **10** QUESTIONS TO COMPLETE WITHIN THE TIME GIVEN.

EXAMPLE

Comprehension Example

Before the dreadful accident, the train with its torn seats had rusty window frames and a multitude of spots of chewing gum which covered its worn-out floors. Now looking at the mangled wreck, passengers, who complained about the strange metallic smell, were lucky to have escaped with no injuries.

Example 1

According to the passage, what seems to have had happened to the train?

A   It was dirty
B   It was unpleasant to ride in
C   It was involved in an accident
D   It was scrapped as it was old

The correct answer is C.

STOP AND WAIT FOR FURTHER INSTRUCTIONS

(c) 2020 Roselle Thompson   11+ Exam English Preparation Tests

Rosa Parks – an Inspiration

Many people around the world have learnt about Rosa Parks' life story because she has become the symbol of freedom and equality to many. Rosa Louise McCauley was an African-American woman who was born in Alabama on 4th February 1913. Her mother was a teacher and her father a carpenter. She had a younger brother named Sylvester. Although her parents separated while she was young, Rosa, her brother and mother went to live with her grandparents, who owned a farm in a town called Pine Level, Montgomery County, Alabama.

During her childhood, the city of Montgomery was segregated, meaning that things were different for white people and black people. They had different schools, different churches, and different stores; had to take different lifts and even drank from different water fountains. Places often had signs saying, "**For Coloreds Only**" or "**For Whites Only**". This meant that Rosa could only attend a poorly equipped school for African-American children. However, her mother being a school teacher, wanted to make sure that Rosa got a high school education. When Rosa rode on buses, she would have to sit in the back; in the seats marked **"For Coloreds."** Sometimes she would have to stand, even if there were seats empty in front. However, despite this discrimination, Rosa attended Montgomery Industrial School for Girls, then the Alabama State Teacher's College. Unfortunately, Rosa's education was cut short, when her mother became very ill, so she left school to care for her mum.

A few years later, she met Raymond Parks, a successful barber, who was working in Montgomery. They married a year later and working part-time, Rosa went back to school, where she finally achieved her High School Diploma.

But life was full of suffering for Rosa who had to live with racism and fear. She was scared of the members of the KKK who had burned down black schools and churches. She also saw a black man being beaten by a white bus driver for getting in his way! Rose and her husband wanted to do something about it. They joined the NAACP, (National Association for the Advancement of Colored People), an organisation that would fight for equal rights and justice for African-Americans in the USA.

This gave Rosa the opportunity to do something about inequality. She attended and led many demonstrations and the one action that she is well-remembered for today, is when she refused to give up her seat on 1st December 1955, to a white man who boarded the bus she was on. The driver told Rosa and other African-Americans on the bus to stand up. Rosa refused. She had a hard day at work, tired, hungry, and exhausted; she decided enough was enough - she refused to stand because she was tired of being treated as a second-class citizen. The police was called, they showed up and Rosa was arrested. She was fined $10 for breaking the segregation law but she refused to pay the fine too. As far as Rosa was concerned, she was not guilty because the law was illegal.

This action caught the attention of African American leaders, In particular Dr. Martin Luther King Jr. African-American people all over Montgomery were outraged at what had happened and decided that they would boycott city buses and walk to work instead. This boycott went on for over a year, (381 days), until finally the US Supreme Court ruled that the segregation laws in Alabama were illegal. Among her many inspirational quotes she left us, Rosa Parks believed that *"each person must live their life as a model to others."*

CONTINUE WORKING

Questions

1. **According to paragraph 1 what is the name Rosa Parks linked to?**
   a. A person who loves animals
   b. Someone who is generous
   c. A role model for freedom and equality
   d. Someone who is wealthy and generous

2. **Which parent would have had a big influence on the young Rosa Parks?**
   a. Her uncles and aunts
   b. Her mother and grandmother
   c. Her brother Sylvester
   d. Her father and his friends

3. **What did the word segregation mean for Rosa and her family?**
   a. They could only go where they were allowed to
   b. They could go anywhere they pleased
   c. They were not really discriminated against
   d. They could ride on buses that were meant for them

4. **Where was the sign saying "For Coloreds only" placed?**
   a. At the front of the bus next to the driver
   b. At the back of the bus
   c. Painted on the sides of buses
   d. On the seats reserved for blacks

5. **Why was Rosa's education interrupted?**
   a. She fell in love with Raymond Parks
   b. Her brother started his own business
   c. Her mother became ill and needed help
   d. Rose decided that she should stop school

6. **What did Rosa achieve at school that would have pleased her mother?**
   a. A High School Diploma
   b. A scholarship to go to a special school
   c. A High School Certificate of Education
   d. A special Diploma from College

7. **What kind of fears did Rosa have to live with? Circle 2**
   a. Not getting a seat on a bus
   b. Threats to her life from the KKK
   c. Their schools and churches being burnt
   d. Their neighbours' angry dogs

8. **What was the reason why a black man was beaten by a white bus driver?**
   a. He was eating food on his bus
   b. He refused to stand up for others
   c. The black man got in his way
   d. He was playing loud music on the bus

CONTINUE WORKING

9. **What role did the NAACP play during this time in America?**
   a. The created shelters for African-Americans
   b. They fought for justice and equal Rights
   c. They attacked the non African-Americans
   d. They made the situation worse

10. **How did the boycott of the buses make a difference to segregation?**
   CIRCLE 2 STATEMENTS
   a. A new law made segregation illegal
   b. The bus drivers were very happy
   c. It created strong unity between African-Americans
   d. The bus companies made more money

STOP AND WAIT FOR FURTHER INSTRUCTIONS

Shuffled Sentences

 **INSTRUCTIONS**

YOU HAVE 8 MINUTES TO COMPLETE THE FOLLOWING SECTION

YOU HAVE 15 QUESTIONS TO COMPLETE WITHIN THE TIME GIVEN.

EXAMPLES

Example 1

The following sentence is shuffled and also contains one unnecessary word. Rearrange the sentence correctly in order to identify the unnecessary word.

Train did time on arrive is not the ran.

A	B	C	D	E
work	ran	morning	try	office

The correct answer is B.

Example 2

Someone door the waited the rang for they to farm open bell and

A	B	C	D	E
home	stood	closed	farm	inside

The correct answer is D.

STOP AND WAIT FOR FURTHER INSTRUCTIONS

Shuffled Sentences

These sentences are shuffled and also contain one unnecessary word. Rearrange them correctly in order to identify the word that's unnecessary.

1. In will airport two must plane we depart our hurry hours

A	B	C	D	E
plane	in	airport	our	must

2. To the late we children their house going friend's house

A	B	C	D	E
we	late	house	their	the

3. Food train we central to yesterday all took London the

A	B	C	D	E
all	to	food	we	the

4. His books two went to library friends Aran went the

A	B	C	D	E
books	webt	the	his	two

5. The old be to years Derek weekend ten at the doing

A	B	C	D	E
at	ten	doing	on	the

6. Next later stop we getting will at said be she off the

A	B	C	D	E
later	we	said	at	off

7. Him his about class his the class change taught change

A	B	C	D	E
his	the	about	him	class

CONTINUE WORKING

8. Her note my plants water me neighbour all reminded to

A	B	C	D	E
to	her	all	me	note

9. Fun weather a fair at gold bought fish we local the

A	B	C	D	E
a	the	at	we	weather

10. Magazine on her pages read work Laura way the to

A	B	C	D	E
her	pages	on	read	to

11. Painter chose the paint my chose yellow my for

A	B	C	D	E
for	the	my	painter	paint

12. The dress time costume party mum fancy made my for

A	B	C	D	E
time	mum	dress	for	my

13. A back week their barbecue had garden in they

A	B	C	D	E
week	a	their	back	they

14. Left comments my wrote book in teacher my several

A	B	C	D	E
my	wrote	left	in	wrote

15. Our night mum special making supper is for something

A	B	C	D	E
our	night	for	something	special

STOP AND WAIT FOR FURTHER INSTRUCTIONS

Synonyms

INSTRUCTIONS

YOU HAVE 7 MINUTES TO COMPLETE THE FOLLOWING SECTION

YOU HAVE 24 QUESTIONS TO COMPLETE WITHIN THE TIME GIVEN.

EXAMPLES

Example 1

Select the word that is most similar in meaning to the following word:

tranquil

A	B	C	D	E
rowdy	windy	quite	peaceful	reach

The correct answer is D.

Example 2

Select the word that is most similar in meaning to the following word:

humorous

A	B	C	D	E
humble	peculiar	holy	comic	creative

The correct answer is C.

STOP AND WAIT FOR FURTHER INSTRUCTIONS

Synonyms

There are 24 questions to complete in this time. You have 7 minutes to complete this section.

Select the word from the table that is most similar in meaning to the word above the table.

1. plan

A	B	C	D	E
please	plot	softly	plead	treat

2. indicate

A	B	C	D	E
show	believe	think	clamp	ticket

3. demolish

A	B	C	D	E
detain	develop	wreck	abundant	report

4. gash

A	B	C	D	E
garage	gush	gestures	cut	carry

5. concept

A	B	C	D	E
control	pleasure	forgive	idea	connect

6. recount

A	B	C	D	E
peaceful	replace	prosper	refrain	tell

7. scrutinise

A	B	C	D	E
scruples	inspect	interesting	co-orporate	central

8. clamorous

A	B	C	D	E
placate	clemency	noisy	supportive	guilty

CONTINUE WORKING

9. uncouth

A	B	C	D	E
strange	sober	intrepid	deceive	scatter

10. peruse

A	B	C	D	E
accept	examine	wander	persuade	permanent

11. justify

A	B	C	D	E
defeat	unite	flexible	choose	explain

12. anecdote

A	B	C	D	E
report	repair	annual	story	stamina

13. define

A	B	C	D	E
definite	strength	explain	depress	dangle

14. bizarre

A	B	C	D	E
peculiar	harsh	bungle	business	bury

15. convention

A	B	C	D	E
central	conclusion	repetition	diversity	custom

16. sweltering

A	B	C	D	E
swipe	heated	freedom	casual	atmosphere

17. possess

A	B	C	D	E
have	perform	proceed	lead	need

18. fade

A	B	C	D	E
disappear	fabricate	fake	higher	consume

CONTINUE WORKING

19. recall

A	B	C	D	E
repeat	remind	remember	restore	reclaim

20. fracture

A	B	C	D	E
rapture	factual	clarity	retain	break

21. slay

A	B	C	D	E
kill	dragon	slide	coach	slate

22. deceased

A	B	C	D	E
focus	dead	increase	credited	insist

23. ample

A	B	C	D	E
assistant	sample	enough	sedate	several

24. blueprint

A	B	C	D	E
plan	colour	shape	pattern	think

STOP AND WAIT FOR FURTHER INSTRUCTIONS

Grammar

⚠️ INSTRUCTIONS

YOU HAVE 5 MINUTES TO COMPLETE THE FOLLOWING SECTION

YOU HAVE 8 QUESTIONS TO COMPLETE WITHIN THE TIME GIVEN.

EXAMPLES

Example 1 - Select the word from the boxes below that is **misspelt**

A	B	C	D	E
lifes	open	sweet	repeat	bishop

The correct answer is A.

Example 2 - Select the correct **prefix or suffix** below to give the opposite to the word *mature.*

A	B	C	D	E
in	il	im	re	non

The correct answer is C.

STOP AND WAIT FOR FURTHER INSTRUCTIONS

1. Select the **Past tense** for the word **"cut"** from the words below.

A	B	C	D	E
cut	grew	think	crop	continue

2. Select the **Homophone** for the word **"ewe"** from the words below.

A	B	C	D	E
welcome	wise	you	yield	swallow

3. Identify the **Antonym** for the word **"admit."**

A	B	C	D	E
tried	deny	adverb	supply	admission

4. Select the word that is **misspelt**.

A	B	C	D	E
embarass	forgiveness	humility	tranquil	assembly

5. Identify the **Simile** for the word **"busy."**

A	B	C	D	E
swarm	park	branch	bee	yellow

6. Identify the **Comparative** for the word **"good."**

A	B	C	D	E
gooder	unwell	better	sick	improve

7. Identify the **Past participle** for the word **"shake"** from the words below.

A	B	C	D	E
shook	shade	shaky	swallow	shaken

8. Identify the **Antonym** for the word **"abundance"** from the words below.

A	B	C	D	E
fragrance	scarce	full	scared	ability

STOP AND WAIT FOR FURTHER INSTRUCTIONS

Antonyms

⚠ INSTRUCTIONS

🕐 YOU HAVE **5** MINUTES TO COMPLETE THE FOLLOWING SECTION

YOU HAVE **15** QUESTIONS TO COMPLETE WITHIN THE TIME GIVEN.

EXAMPLES

Example 1

Which word is least similar to the following word:

dark

A	B	C	D	E
night	morning	light	bright	heavy

The correct answer is C.

Example 2

Which word is least similar to the following word:

departure

A	B	C	D	E
entrance	main	rough	arrival	below

The correct answer is D.

STOP AND WAIT FOR FURTHER INSTRUCTIONS ⬡ STOP

Choose a word from each box below, that is opposite to the word in the question:

1. detest

A	B	C	D	E
depend	admire	admit	degrade	assist

2. amuse

A	B	C	D	E
bore	amaze	recall	prepare	funny

3. humble

A	B	C	D	E
halt	jovial	replace	hateful	arrogant

4. bare

A	B	C	D	E
bossy	brim	covered	smoky	basket

5. blunt

A	B	C	D	E
blame	sharp	blouse	mount	misery

6. limited

A	B	C	D	E
limit	restrain	bountiful	boundless	respect

7. brief

A	B	C	D	E
bright	long	reveal	brisk	brought

8. scarce

A	B	C	D	E
scary	plentiful	hinder	reverse	speed

CONTINUE WORKING

9. optimistic

A	B	C	D	E
optical	eclectic	pessimistic	tricky	refusal

10. insult

A	B	C	D	E
compliment	insider	introspect	roast	imply

11. fact

A	B	C	D	E
cite	pact	knight	seize	fiction

12. prey

A	B	C	D	E
practice	praise	goalkeeper	predator	monitor

13. industrious

A	B	C	D	E
lazy	manufacture	create	simply	obstinate

14. adjacent

A	B	C	D	E
adjust	fix	overall	distant	advisor

15. hope

A	B	C	D	E
heartfelt	happiness	despair	drastic	drowsy

STOP AND WAIT FOR FURTHER INSTRUCTIONS

Cloze

# INSTRUCTIONS

YOU HAVE **10** MINUTES TO COMPLETE THE FOLLOWING SECTION

YOU HAVE **20** QUESTIONS TO COMPLETE WITHIN THE TIME GIVEN.

EXAMPLES

Example 1

Read the sentence below and select the most appropriate word from the table.

A	B	C	D	E
canopy	canvas	scenery	display	picture

The wall of the abandoned building was the perfect ……………………………for the painter.

Example 2

Read the sentence below and select the most appropriate word from the table.

A	B	C	D	E
send	call	attend	reply	absent

We are expected to …………………………to the wedding invitation before the end of the month.

STOP AND WAIT FOR FURTHER INSTRUCTIONS

Read the passage and select the most appropriate word from the table below.

A	B	C	D	E
world	difficult	thirsty	droughts	Sahara

F	G	H	I	J
nutrients	die	survive	surface	showers

The importance of Water

Absolutely every living thing needs water to (Q1).......................... Our bodies consist of about 75% water. Plants and animals – everything needs this precious transparent liquid every day or we will (Q2).......................... Water covers about two thirds of the total (Q3).......................of the earth. The majority of these surface areas are the seas or oceans which have long been a major source of both food and transport. Our need for water is obvious when we become (Q4)......................and it helps our blood to flow through the blood vessels, transporting vital (Q5)............................to our bodies. Water is used for drinking, washing, cleaning and cooking and is also needed to transport waste matter from our bodies via the excretory system.

The lack of water in parts of the (Q6)............................is keenly felt by plants, animals and humans, and without it, there are deaths, especially during (Q7)......................and famine. Moreover, areas where there is very little rain, like the (Q8).......................... Desert, there is very little growing and this makes it (Q9)...................... for man to live there. For some of us who live in countries where water is plentiful, it's hard to imagine not having water or the luxury of baths and (Q10)............................that we can enjoy for as long as we like.

CONTINUE WORKING

(c) 2020 Roselle Thompson *11+ Exam English Preparation Tests*

Read the passage and select the most appropriate word from the table below.

A	B	C	D	E
chocolates	Norwegian	spy	injuries	recounted

F	G	H	I	J
armchair	American	divorced	legacy	inspire

Roald Dahl

Children, who often read books, would usually quote one of Roald Dahl's books as their favourite books. Roald Dahl wrote many of his books in a shed in his garden, sitting on an old battered (Q11).......................... He was born in Llandaff, Wales on 13th September 1916 to (Q12).................... parents. He was sent to boarding school and many of the bizarre and memorable events of his childhood have been (Q13).................... in his books. Dahl loved (Q14)..........................., and as a child he used to receive packages from Cadbury for him to taste and then give his opinions on the new bars being made. This no doubt helped to (Q15).................... his book *Charlie and the Chocolate Factory*. Roal Dahl's books have sold more than 250 million copies worldwide.

But Dahl was not only a writer, he had a passion for travelling, so he ventured to Canada, then East Africa where he worked for an oil company until World War II broke out. He joined the Royal Air Force when he was 23 years old. In 1940 Dahl's Gladiator aircraft crash-landed in the Western Desert, and he suffered (Q16)..........................to his head, nose and back. After only 6 months Dahl was back in action; this time in the Battle of Athens, before he became a British (Q17)..........................to MI6.

In 1953, he married an (Q18)............................actress, Patricia Neal, with whom he had 5 children. Their marriage lasted 30 until they (Q19)...........................and he married his second wife Felicity "Liccy". Dahl died at the age of 74, on 23 November 1990. He left behind his amazing (Q20)....................of books together with his Roald Dahl Museum and Story Centre which continue to inspire millions of children today.

STOP AND WAIT FOR FURTHER INSTRUCTIONS

Answer Sheet – Paper 5

(c) 2020 Roselle Thompson — 11+ Exam English Preparation Tests

This is a multiple-choice answer sheet with the following sections:

COMPREHENSION (questions 1–10): options A B C D E

SYNONYMS (questions 10–24): options A B C D E (questions 15–19 have options A B C D E; questions 20–24 have options A B C D E)

GRAMMAR (questions 1–8): options A B C D E

SHUFFLED SENTENCES (questions 1–15): options A B C D E

ANTONYMS (questions 1–15): options A B C D E

CLOZE (questions 1–20): choose from letters A B C D E F G H I J

SYNONYMS (questions 1–9): options A B C D E

Instructions: Shade the correct answer box. If the answer is **D** then shade **D**.

Example: A | B | C | [D]

ANSWERS TO TEST - PAPER 1

Comprehension

Q1   C - imagined
Q2   B - foreign
Q3   B - tactic
Q4   C - bongo drums
Q5   B - execute
Q6   C - like a hare
Q7   E - it was raining
Q8   C - instincts
Q9   B - dead
Q10 D - he had lung cancer

Shuffled Sentences

Q1   B – *dry*
Despite the forecast of wet weather we still had a barbecue.
Q2   A – *home*
We booked tickets to see the latest film.
Q3   E – *although*
The dog ran to fetch the stick for its owner.
Q4   B – *weather*
The news reported a hurricane had damaged the island.
Q5   D – *time*
He was late for his interview so he ran to catch the bus.
Q6   B – *took*
Many tourists went on a river boat cruise on the Thames.
Q7   A – *day*
The black dog barked at the neighbour's playful cat.
Q8   B – *builder*
We had a new shower installed in our bathroom.
Q9   E – *uncomfortable*
She sat up in bed propped by two pillows.
Q10 B – *cried*
The children screamed loudly on the scary ride.
Q11 A – *fast*
The horse trotted around the field with its new rider.
Q12 C – *garden*
The boy kicked the ball which broke his neighbour's window.
Q13 B – *heavy*
An accident caused a traffic jam on the motorway.
Q14 A – *England*
The current British monarch is Queen Elizabeth II.
Q15 D – *bright*
The flowers looked beautiful in their glass vase

Synonyms		Grammar	
Q1	A – transparent	Q1	B - so
Q2	B – calm	Q2	B - curiosity
Q3	E – begin	Q3	D - waist
Q4	B – delicate	Q4	A - acquire
Q5	E – bendable	Q5	D - strong
Q6	D – lots	Q6	A - example
Q7	A – intricate	Q7	D - happy
Q8	E – motivating	Q8	A - committee
Q9	E – sufficient		
Q10	B – rely	**Antonyms**	
Q11	D – fascinated	Q1	E - above
Q12	C – rude	Q2	A - defeat
Q13	C – speed	Q3	B - transparent
Q14	C - mimic	Q4	D - unimportant
Q15	E – positive	Q5	C - allow
Q16	B - cunning	Q6	A - scorn
Q17	C – declare	Q7	A - individual
Q18	B – anger	Q8	B - discourage
Q19	C – crowd	Q9	C - indolent
Q20	E – peaceful	Q10	C - spendthrift
Q21	D – scatter	Q11	B - scarce
Q22	C – dodge	Q12	D - polite
Q23	C - friendly	Q13	A - disobey
Q24	C – cure	Q14	D - distant
		Q15	C - inaudible

Cloze

Q1	J – existence	Q11	G – memorable
Q2	F – buried	Q12	E - designer
Q3	H – paintings	Q13	J – antiques
Q4	A – ledges	Q14	B – curious
Q5	E – Archaeologists	Q15	C – London
Q6	I – sides	Q16	F – Doomsday
Q7	D – mystery	Q17	I – stroll
Q8	C – first	Q18	A – buzz
Q9	B – structures	Q19	D - diversity
Q10	G – Wonders	Q20	H - discoveries

(c) 2020 Roselle Thompson *11+ Exam English Preparation Tests*

ANSWERS TO TEST - PAPER 2

Comprehension

Q1   C
Q2   C
Q3   A & C
Q4   B
Q5   B
Q6   A & D
Q7   D
Q8   C
Q9   B
Q10 C

Shuffled Sentences

Q1   C – *get*
They closed all the shops because of a dangerous virus.

Q2   E – *clock*
Tom picked Mary up from the train station at 8pm.

Q3   B – *for*
My neighbour walked his two dogs in our local park.

Q4   A – *broken*
The glass shattered into fragments when it hit the floor.

Q5   D – *home*
They called the ambulance for the sick man in the Centre.

Q6   B – *school*
We were only allowed to play after we did our homework.

Q7   A – *rainbow*
The colourful garden flowers looked beautiful in the rain.

Q8   C – *local*
The Council closed the outdoor market because of the windy weather.

Q9   E – *bike*
Jane bought a strong lock for her locker at the Gym.

Q10 D – *station*
Ivan went to pick up his blue car from the local garage.

Q11 B – *cry*
Jack made funny faces so the whole class laughed.

Q12 A – *room*
We found many coins behind our soft grey sofa.

Q13 D – *green*
She cried because she did not want to eat the peas on her plate.

Q14 C – *on*
Sarah made her mum cross when she did not clean her room.

Q15 E – *ancient*
He apologised for breaking mum's special Chinese vase.

Synonyms

Q1	C – strong
Q2	E – hide
Q3	B – lazy
Q4	C – soon
Q5	A – begin
Q6	D – obstruct
Q7	C – show
Q8	D – cure
Q9	B – fast
Q10	C – forbid
Q11	D – annual
Q12	E – flexible
Q13	B – rowdy
Q14	C – choice
Q15	D – feeble
Q16	A – bravery
Q17	C – yield
Q18	D – join
Q19	B – obstinate
Q20	C – omen
Q21	D – empty
Q22	B – strong
Q23	E – peaceful
Q24	C – harsh

Grammar

Q1	B – reign
Q2	A – ability
Q3	E – Ireland
Q4	A – accompany
Q5	D – slim
Q6	A – excite
Q7	D – copy
Q8	B – humorous

Antonyms

Q1	D – fake
Q2	E – bless
Q3	A – hide
Q4	C – peace
Q5	C – moving
Q6	B – prohibit
Q7	C – secret
Q8	E – sure
Q9	B – temporary
Q10	E – love
Q11	A – end
Q12	E – ancient
Q13	B – contract
Q14	D – passive
Q15	A – destroy

Cloze

Q1	C – rainfall		Q11	I – generations
Q2	E – surface		Q12	D – preserved
Q3	A – species		Q13	A – supernatural
Q4	H – hot		Q14	G – versions
Q5	J – equator		Q15	E – cultures
Q6	G – temperate		Q16	I – miracles
Q7	B – branches		Q17	B – existed
Q8	D – undergrowth		Q18	F – century
Q9	I – endangered		Q19	H – sword
Q10	F – deforestation		Q20	C – lesson

ANSWERS TO TEST - PAPER 3

Comprehension

- Q1   C - Syon House, Hampton Court Palace, Richmond Hill, Kew
- Q2   A - Cotswolds
- Q3   B – 43AD
- Q4   D – A Frost Fair
- Q5   B – less pillars in the water
- Q6   B & D
- Q7   A & D
- Q8   D – 691 people
- Q9   B & C
- Q10 A & D

Shuffled Sentences

- Q1   A– Ben
  Patrick took his dog to the vet at the weekend.
- Q2   C – *play*
  The children made a tent with cardboard.
- Q3   D – *bread*
  The fatal road accident caused a traffic jam.
- Q4   B – *weekend*
  Mum took us to the swimming pool for an hour.
- Q5   E – *sausages*
  We had a barbecue after we swept all the leaves in the garden.
- Q6   A – *Saturday*
  A local builder built our garden fence at the weekend.
- Q7   D – *morning*
  Tom got detention for not doing his homework yesterday.
- Q8   B – *drink*
  Derek loves food but hates gerkin in his hamburger.
- Q9   C – *lessons*
  The rain fell heavily all day so we stayed in during break-time.
- Q10 B – *last*
  Firemen were called to put out a fire at the Shopping Centre
- Q11 A – *Palace*
  Many tourists visit London during the summer months.
- Q12 D – *time*
  The boy struggled to ride his bike up a hill.
- Q13 D – *weekend*
  The children went camping with their school.
- Q14 C – *Monday*
  Jack promised to read his new book before the end of the week.
- Q15 E – *soon*
  They waited for the postman to arrive with their new PS4 game.

Synonyms

Q1	C – help
Q2	A – fake
Q3	C – hang
Q4	D – inactive
Q5	B – slope
Q6	C – distant
Q7	B – show
Q8	D – scanty
Q9	E – disaster
Q10	A – protect
Q11	A – brave
Q12	B – feel
Q13	D – loving
Q14	C – high
Q15	C – understand
Q16	B – enemy
Q17	D – deceive
Q18	B – dusk
Q19	A – gather
Q20	B – clothes
Q21	C – gain
Q22	C – enough
Q23	B – persuade
Q24	E – scatter

Grammar

Q1	D - slow
Q2	B - groan
Q3	D - fertile
Q4	A - generosity
Q5	C - holy
Q6	A - descend
Q7	B - theirs
Q8	D - miserable

Antonyms

Q1	B - bold
Q2	E - superior
Q3	A - pass
Q4	C - deep
Q5	D - win
Q6	A - innocent
Q7	C - drunk
Q8	E - fresh
Q9	C - wild
Q10	C - wane
Q11	B - accept
Q12	E - junior
Q13	C - captive
Q14	C - majority
Q15	A - employer

Cloze

Q1	H – globe		Q11	F – siblings
Q2	A – million		Q12	E - alerted
Q3	I – world		Q13	B – nudge
Q4	G – matured		Q14	G – shrugged
Q5	B – climate		Q15	I – tiptoed
Q6	F – ingredient		Q16	D – stiffly
Q7	E – mass		Q17	A – clasped
Q8	C – bitter		Q18	J – suspicious
Q9	J – nutritional		Q19	C - disbelief
Q10	D – darker		Q20	H - neighbourhood

ANSWERS TO TEST - PAPER 4

Comprehension

- Q1   D - in a coach
- Q2   B – they have been crying
- Q3   C – 11am
- Q4   B – excited and loving
- Q5   C – her son had left his toy behind
- Q6   C – on the pavement opposite the coach
- Q7   D - embarrassed
- Q8   D – running out of the coach
- Q9   A – they laughed at the boy
- Q10   B – he feels ashamed and wishes his mum could go away

Shuffled Sentences

- Q1   A– *long*
  The children played in their swimming pool all day.
- Q2   C – *stick*
  The dog buried his bone in the corner of our garden.
- Q3   C – *morning*
  The fatal road accident caused a traffic jam.
- Q4   B – *train*
  Dad took us to see the new pandas at London Zoo.
- Q5   D – *into*
  We all ran out of the class when the fire alarm went off.
- Q6   E – *fast*
  All trains to London were cancelled due to bad weather.
- Q7   A – *yesterday*
  She needs black ink for her new printer.
- Q8   E – *animals*
  The farmer gave us extra milk and cheese when we visited him.
- Q9   C – *today*
  There is a lot to see at Madam Tussauds at any time.
- Q10   A – *not*
  It is unsafe to eat meat which is uncooked.
- Q11   D – *tigers*
  We studied plenty of interesting wildlife in science.
- Q12   B – *future*
  Scientists believe the temperature of the earth is increasing.
- Q13   C – *borrow*
  She prefers to carry her gloves rather than wear them.
- Q14   D – *costume*
  A wedding event is a great opportunity to dress up.
- Q15   B – *reason*
  Her parents gave her permission to go out.

Synonyms		Grammar	
Q1	C – lie	Q1	C - rung
Q2	B – start	Q2	C - lightening
Q3	C – huge	Q3	B - generous
Q4	C – outdated	Q4	A - committee
Q5	E – fake	Q5	D - air
Q6	D – untrue	Q6	E - least
Q7	D – hurriedly	Q7	A - that
Q8	B – usual	Q8	A - either
Q9	E – novice		
Q10	A – large	**Antonyms**	
Q11	C – unsafe	Q1	E - scatter
Q12	A – ugly	Q2	A - stand
Q13	C – brave	Q3	D - horizontal
Q14	A – notorious	Q4	C - moving
Q15	E – decorative	Q5	D - passenger
Q16	B – speed	Q6	E - guest
Q17	C – achieve	Q7	C - liquid
Q18	C – obtain	Q8	D - advance
Q19	A – keep	Q9	D - peace
Q20	E – reveal	Q10	D - flow
Q21	B – fall	Q11	D - fine
Q22	B – settle	Q12	B - sweet
Q23	C – choose	Q13	E - straight
Q24	E – accumulate	Q14	D - strong
		Q15	C - poverty

Cloze

Q1	G – attractions	Q11	F – access
Q2	J – imprisoned	Q12	H – communication
Q3	C – intervened	Q13	C – purchases
Q4	B – inherited	Q14	J – inaccessible
Q5	A – Europe	Q15	A – procedure
Q6	H – exhibition	Q16	B – transfer
Q7	D – Baker	Q17	D – filling
Q8	I – fire	Q18	G – transactions
Q9	E – bombings	Q19	I – programs
Q10	F – Royal	Q20	E – emitted

ANSWERS TO TEST - PAPER 5

Comprehension

Q1   C
Q2   B
Q3   A
Q4   D
Q5   C
Q6   A
Q7   B & C
Q8   C
Q9   A
Q10   A & C

Shuffled Sentences

Q1   **C –** *airport*
We must hurry; our plane will depart in two hours.

Q2   **B –** *late*
The children are going to their friend'shouse today.

Q3   **C –** *food*
Yesterday we all took the train to Central London.

Q4   **A –** *books*
Aran went to the library with his two friends.

Q5   **D –** *on*
Derek is going to be ten years old at the weekend.

Q6   **A –** *later*
She said we will be getting off at the next stop.

Q7   **D –** *him*
His teacher taught the class about climate change.

Q8   **E –** *note*
My neighbour reminded me to water all her plants.

Q9   **E –** *weather*
We bought a gold fish at the local fun fair.

Q10   **B –** *pages*
Laura read her magazine on the way to work.

Q11   **D –** *painter*
I chose the yellow paint for my bedroom.

Q12   **A –** *time*
Mum made my costume for the fancy dress party.

Q13   **A –** *week*
They had a barbecue in their back garden.

Q14   **C –** *left*
My teacher wrote several comments in my book.

Q15   **B –** *night*
Mum is making something special for our supper.

Synonyms

Q1	B – plot
Q2	A – show
Q3	C – wreck
Q4	D – cut
Q5	D – idea
Q6	E – tell
Q7	B – inspect
Q8	C – noisy
Q9	A – strange
Q10	B – examine
Q11	E – explain
Q12	D – story
Q13	C – explain
Q14	A – peculiar
Q15	E – custom
Q16	B – heated
Q17	A – have
Q18	A – disappear
Q19	C – remember
Q20	E – break
Q21	A – kill
Q22	B – dead
Q23	C – enough
Q24	A – plan

Grammar

Q1	A - cut
Q2	C - you
Q3	B - deny
Q4	A - embarrass
Q5	D - bee
Q6	C - better
Q7	E - shaken
Q8	B - scarce

Antonyms

Q1	B - admire
Q2	A - bore
Q3	E - arrogant
Q4	C - covered
Q5	B - sharp
Q6	D - boundless
Q7	B - long
Q8	B - plentiful
Q9	C - pessimistic
Q10	A - compliment
Q11	E - fiction
Q12	D - predator
Q13	A - lazy
Q14	D - distant
Q15	C - despair

Cloze

Q1	H – survive		Q11	F – armchair
Q2	G – die		Q12	B – Norwegian
Q3	I – surface		Q13	E – recounted
Q4	C – thirsty		Q14	A – chocolates
Q5	F – nutrients		Q15	J – inspire
Q6	A – world		Q16	D – injuries
Q7	D – drought		Q17	C – spy
Q8	E – Sahara		Q18	G – American
Q9	B – difficult		Q19	H - divorced
Q10	J – showers		Q20	I - legacy

About the Author

Roselle Thompson B.A Hons, MPhil, FRSA, has over 27 years of experience in teaching and education development in the UK, from nursery to University levels. In addition to her academic lecturing and writing, Roselle is an Author, Poet, Playwright, Editor and Broadcaster, who has been creating, since 1994, intensive courses in a number of subjects; including English (language and literature), Verbal Reasoning and Public Speaking for children from as young as 5 years old, to GCSE Secondary and A level 6th Form. Roselle also organises extra support Tutorials for Undergraduates struggling in their first year at university. As a Broadcaster and International Speaker and Poet, her approach is therefore to make her significantly accumulated skills available to her students for their personal empowerment, development and life-long success.

BOOKS IN THE SERIES, BY THE SAME AUTHOR...............

ENGLISH GRAMMAR: A STUDENT'S COMPANION

This book prepares children for the **11+ independent** and State **grammar schools** as well as the **Key Stage 2 SATs tests** and **Common Entrance** at 13 years. Although there are a variety of grammar books on the market, this book is based on over 27 years of the Author's techniques based on teaching, heading schools and rigorously tested exercises done in both school and tuition classrooms. The book contains a thorough preparation in grammar, and has valuable **exercises for all aspects of foundation English literacy development** to **secondary level** education and **beyond**. **The Book is divided into 6 sections with Learning Targets, Focus and Assessment indicators and 145 Test exercises, with Answers.** Each section includes work which **combines reading and writing skills to meet pupils' learning targets.**

VOCABULARY SKILLS FOR PRACTICAL LEARNING

The Vocabulary book contains over **60 Units** and **60 Unit Tests** which can be used as lessons, **with a total of 600 vocabulary words.** Each Unit presents at least 10 vocabulary words which show their class or part of speech, together with their definition. This is followed by **60 gap-filling worksheet exercises** for you to complete, without looking at the meaning. Each gap-filling exercise helps students to see how these words are used in their contexts and tests the child's knowledge of them. Check out the **39 general knowledge challenges** set throughout the book as well as **16 interesting brain-teasing crossword puzzles!**

SPELLING & WORD POWER SKILLS

The books in the **Spelling & Word-Power Series** cover **3 levels of practice**, arranged from **Starters** (which introduces the structure of words, sounds and rules), **Level 1** (expands knowledge of phonics and increases the level of structuring of words and rules which guide them), **Level 2** and **Level 3** (provides more challenges in exercises and rules. **Rules** are identified and practice is given in exercises that test understanding. **Practice exercises** for you to complete, test your understanding of the rules applied. In this book, to help you spell correctly, there are spelling strategies that look at the certain aspects of the **sound, structure and spelling of words.** Additionally, some **word-hunt challenges** help you to become aware of the origin of words, forcing a closer look at the rules and word formation.

MASTERING COMPREHENSION SKILLS

This book provides a complete package of introduction, revision and practice comprehension passages to help you with preparation for the Key Stage SATSs tests and those preparing for the 11+ independent and State Grammar School, Common Entrance exams at 13+ and preparation for GCSE English Language Paper 1.
The passages cover work in Key Stage Two, Three and Four of the National Curriculum and beyond. **The texts in this book have been carefully selected to be age-appropriate and cover a range of text types.** The format of the questions replicates the Reading and Comprehension components of the tests to help your child become familiar with the exam format and requirements.

Acknowledgements
The Author and Publisher would like to acknowledge use of the following:
The poem entitled *"Letting Go"* from *"Rhythms of Life: An Anthology of Modern Poetry,"* (2019) by Roselle Thompson

www.ingramcontent.com/pod-product-compliance
Lightning Source LLC
Chambersburg PA
CBHW042016090526
44588CB00023B/2879